Battleground Eu

Fort Vaux

**South side of Fort Vaux before
the siege of June 1916.**

Battleground series:

Stamford Bridge & Hastings *by* Peter Marren
Wars of the Roses - **Wakefield / Towton** *by* Philip A. Haigh
Wars of the Roses - **Barnet** *by* David Clark
Wars of the Roses - **Tewkesbury** *by* Steven Goodchild
Wars of the Roses - **The Battles of St Albans** *by*
Peter Burley, Michael Elliott & Harvey Wilson
English Civil War - **Naseby** *by* Martin Marix Evans, Peter Burton
and Michael Westaway
English Civil War - **Marston Moor** *by* David Clark
War of the Spanish Succession - **Blenheim 1704** *by* James Falkner
War of the Spanish Succession - **Ramillies 1706** *by* James Falkner
Napoleonic - **Hougoumont** *by* Julian Paget and Derek Saunders
Napoleonic - **Waterloo** *by* Andrew Uffindell and Michael Corum
Zulu War - **Isandlwana** *by* Ian Knight and Ian Castle
Zulu War - **Rorkes Drift** *by* Ian Knight and Ian Castle
Boer War - **The Relief of Ladysmith** *by* Lewis Childs
Boer War - **The Siege of Ladysmith** *by* Lewis Childs
Boer War - **Kimberley** *by* Lewis Childs

Mons *by* Jack Horsfall and Nigel Cave
Néry *by* Patrick Tackle
Le Cateau *by* Nigel Cave and Jack Shelden
Walking the Salient *by* Paul Reed
Ypres - **Sanctuary Wood and Hooge** *by* Nigel Cave
Ypres - **Hill 60** *by* Nigel Cave
Ypres - **Messines Ridge** *by* Peter Oldham
Ypres - **Polygon Wood** *by* Nigel Cave
Ypres - **Passchendaele** *by* Nigel Cave
Ypres - **Airfields and Airmen** *by* Mike O'Connor
Ypres - **St Julien** *by* Graham Keech
Ypres - **Boesinghe** *by* Stephen McGreal
Walking the Somme *by* Paul Reed
Somme - **Gommecourt** *by* Nigel Cave
Somme - **Serre** *by* Jack Horsfall & Nigel Cave
Somme - **Beaumont Hamel** *by* Nigel Cave
Somme - **Thiepval** *by* Michael Stedman
Somme - **La Boiselle** *by* Michael Stedman
Somme - **Fricourt** *by* Michael Stedman
Somme - **Carnoy-Montauban** *by* Graham Maddocks
Somme - **Pozières** *by* Graham Keech
Somme - **Courcelette** *by* Paul Reed
Somme - **Boom Ravine** *by* Trevor Pidgeon
Somme - **Mametz Wood** *by* Michael Renshaw
Somme - **Delville Wood** *by* Nigel Cave
Somme - **Advance to Victory (North) 1918** *by* Michael Stedman
Somme - **Flers** *by* Trevor Pidgeon
Somme - **Bazentin Ridge** *by* Edward Hancock
Somme - **Combles** *by* Paul Reed
Somme - **Beaucourt** *by* Michael Renshaw
Somme - **Redan Ridge** *by* Michael Renshaw
Somme - **Hamel** *by* Peter Pedersen
Somme - **Villers-Bretonneux** *by* Peter Pedersen
Somme - **Airfields and Airmen** *by* Mike O'Connor
Airfields and Airmen of the Channel Coast *by* Mike O'Connor
In the Footsteps of the Red Baron *by* Mike O'Connor
Arras - **Airfields and Airmen** *by* Mike O'Connor
Arras - **The Battle for Vimy Ridge** *by* Jack Shelden & Nigel Cave
Arras - **Vimy Ridge** *by* Nigel Cave
Arras - **Gavrelle** *by* Trevor Tasker and Kyle Tallett
Arras - **Oppy Wood** *by* David Bilton
Arras - **Bullecourt** *by* Graham Keech
Arras - **Monchy le Preux** *by* Colin Fox
Walking Arras *by* Paul Reed
Hindenburg Line *by* Peter Oldham
Hindenburg Line - **Epehy** *by* Bill Mitchinson
Hindenburg Line - **Riqueval** *by* Bill Mitchinson
Hindenburg Line - **Villers-Plouich** *by* Bill Mitchinson
Hindenburg Line - **Cambrai Right Hook** *by* Jack Horsfall & Nigel Cave
Hindenburg Line - **Cambrai Flesquières** *by* Jack Horsfall & Nigel Cave
Hindenburg Line - **Saint Quentin** *by* Helen McPhail and Philip Guest

Hindenburg Line - **Bourlon Wood** *by* Jack Horsfall & Nigel Cave
Cambrai - **Airfields and Airmen** *by* Mike O'Connor
Aubers Ridge *by* Edward Hancock
La Bassée - **Neuve Chapelle** *by* Geoffrey Bridger
Loos - **Hohenzollern Redoubt** *by* Andrew Rawson
Loos - **Hill 70** *by* Andrew Rawson
Fromelles *by* Peter Pedersen
The Battle of the Lys 1918 *by* Phil Tomaselli
Accrington Pals Trail *by* William Turner
Poets at War: Wilfred Owen *by* Helen McPhail and Philip Guest
Poets at War: Edmund Blunden *by* Helen McPhail and Philip Guest
Poets at War: Graves & Sassoon *by* Helen McPhail and Philip Guest
Gallipoli *by* Nigel Steel
Gallipoli - **Gully Ravine** *by* Stephen Chambers
Gallipoli - **Anzac Landing** *by* Stephen Chambers
Gallipoli - **Suvla August Offensive** *by* Stephen Chambers
Gallipoli - **Landings at Helles** *by* Huw & Jill Rodge
Walking the Italian Front *by* Francis Mackay
Italy - **Asiago** *by* Francis Mackay
Verdun: **Fort Douamont** *by* Christina Holstein
Verdun: **Fort Vaux** *by* Christina Holstein
Walking Verdun *by* Christina Holstein
Zeebrugge & Ostend Raids 1918 *by* Stephen McGreal

Germans at Beaumont Hamel *by* Jack Sheldon
Germans at Thiepval *by* Jack Sheldon

SECOND WORLD WAR

Dunkirk *by* Patrick Wilson
Calais *by* Jon Cooksey
Boulogne *by* Jon Cooksey
Saint-Nazaire *by* James Dorrian
Normandy - **Pegasus Bridge** *by* Carl Shilleto
Normandy - **Merville Battery** *by* Carl Shilleto
Normandy - **Utah Beach** *by* Carl Shilleto
Normandy - **Omaha Beach** *by* Tim Kilvert-Jones
Normandy - **Gold Beach** *by* Christopher Dunphie & Garry Johnson
Normandy - **Gold Beach Jig** *by* Tim Saunders
Normandy - **Juno Beach** *by* Tim Saunders
Normandy - **Sword Beach** *by* Tim Kilvert-Jones
Normandy - **Operation Bluecoat** *by* Ian Daglish
Normandy - **Operation Goodwood** *by* Ian Daglish
Normandy - **Epsom** *by* Tim Saunders
Normandy - **Hill 112** *by* Tim Saunders
Normandy - **Mont Pinçon** *by* Eric Hunt
Normandy - **Cherbourg** *by* Andrew Rawson
Normandy - **Commandos & Rangers on D Day** *by* Tim Saunders
Das Reich - **Drive to Normandy** *by* Philip Vickers
Oradour *by* Philip Beck
Market Garden - **Nijmegen** *by* Tim Saunders
Market Garden - **Hell's Highway** *by* Tim Saunders
Market Garden - **Arnhem, Oosterbeek** *by* Frank Steer
Market Garden - **Arnhem, The Bridge** *by* Frank Steer
Market Garden - **The Island** *by* Tim Saunders
Rhine Crossing - **US 9th Army & 17th US Airborne** *by* Andrew Rawson
British Rhine Crossing – Operation Varsity *by* Tim Saunders
British Rhine Crossing – Operation Plunder *by* Tim Saunders
Battle of the Bulge – St Vith *by* Michael Tolhurst
Battle of the Bulge – Bastogne *by* Michael Tolhurst
Channel Islands *by* George Forty
Walcheren *by* Andrew Rawson
Remagen Bridge *by* Andrew Rawson
Cassino *by* Ian Blackwell
Anzio *by* Ian Blackwell
Dieppe *by* Tim Saunders
Fort Eben Emael *by* Tim Saunders
Crete – The Airborne Invasion *by* Tim Saunders
Malta *by* Paul Williams

Battleground Europe

Fort Vaux

Christina Holstein

First World War Series Editor
Nigel Cave

Pen & Sword
MILITARY

First published in Great Britain in 2011 by
Pen & Sword Military an imprint of
Pen & Sword Books Ltd
47 Church Street
Barnsley
South Yorkshire
S70 2AS
Copyright © Christina Holstein

ISBN 9781848843578

Typeset in Times New Roman PS 10pt by
Pen & Sword Books Ltd
Printed and bound in the United Kingdom by
CPI Group (UK) Ltd, Croydon, CR0 4YY

Pen & Sword Books Ltd incorporates the Imprints of Pen & Sword
Aviation, Pen & Sword Maritime, Pen & Sword Military, Wharncliffe
Local History, Pen and Sword Select, Pen and Sword Military
Classics and Leo Cooper.
For a complete list of Pen & Sword titles please contact
PEN & SWORD BOOKS LIMITED
47 Church Street, Barnsley, South Yorkshire, S70 2AS, England
E-mail: enquiries@pen-and-sword.co.uk
Website: www.pen-and-sword.co.uk

CONTENTS

Introduction by Series Editor 6
Author's Note 8
Introduction 10
Advice to Tourers 13
List of Maps and Plans 16

Chapter 1 **A Trapezium of Modest Size** **17**
Chapter 2 **To Take Fort Vaux This Very Day** **29**
Chapter 3 **Major Raynal Takes Command** **43**
Chapter 4 **The Siege Begins** **57**
Chapter 5 **A Problem With Water** **75**
Chapter 6 **Surrender** **95**
Chapter 7 **Fort Vaux Returns to French Hands** **117**

TOUR No. 1: Fort Vaux Outside **135**
TOUR No. 2: Fort Vaux Inside **151**
TOUR No. 3: A Walk in the Vaux sector **164**
TOUR No. 4: A Driving Tour around French Rear Areas **177**

Select Bibliography 195
Further Reading 197
Short Glossary 199
Useful Addresses 199
Battlefield Sites 200
Grave Location 202
Archives 202
Acknowledgements 203
Index 204

**The price of battle:
German prisoners of war
carry French wounded away.**

INTRODUCTION BY SERIES EDITOR

This is Christina Holstein's third *Battleground Europe* book on Verdun, the first two of which have been models of the type, packed with clear information, placing events and the significance of features under discussion clearly into context, and providing a coherent explanation of what happened through a gripping narrative and a skilful use of contemporary accounts and memoirs. This is all supported by excellent, meticulous and informative tours and detailed mapping. Fort Vaux is a worthy addition to her work thus far on Verdun. It is somewhat strange that the best guides to this battlefield (in my opinion – and in that of many others) happen to be in English and perhaps this is symptomatic of a curious lack of wider national interest in the haunting remains of the gargantuan clash on these heights above the Meuse.

Verdun had been brought to life for me by the beautifully written book by Alistair Horne, *The Price of Glory: Verdun 1916*, which is still in print and remains a sound introduction to the subject, even though some of the interpretations and factual elements have been challenged over the decades since it was first published. The story in it of the fighting for Fort Vaux epitomized many aspects of the horrendous battle – the longest of the Great War – that was Verdun 1916. Courage,

Shell damage on the south side of Fort Vaux, close to the Eastern Bourges Casemate. This postcard view was taken before June 1916. *Tom Gudmestad*

endurance, existing – let alone fighting – in truly ghastly conditions, tenacity, comradeship and perseverance: all of these attributes applied to so many who fought here. Any verbal description could not hope to match the reality on the ground for the men of France and Germany who died or were mutilated in their hundreds and thousands as they sought to secure possession of the fort and its immediate surroundings.

One of the strange things about Verdun, at least to me, is how relatively poorly presented this battlefield is, especially given its seminal place in French history and its endurance as a symbol that is frequently used in France's developing relationship with Germany. True, there is a good museum at Fleury; true, more explanatory plaques have appeared over the recent years, yet ... For most visitors, Verdun is Fleury and Fort Douaumont (and even the latter could be better presented, one feels). We should acknowledge the hard work put in by local associations to keep the flame lit, but they cannot be expected to do everything on their own.

Fort Vaux is off the beaten tourist trail, and Christina sounds some melancholy notes – plaques stolen or destroyed, and the air of decay and neglect hanging over the fort. It was ever a doom-laden place – as might be said of the whole battlefield – and I certainly felt that atmosphere during my first visit of some twenty-five years ago.

'Over the years tourist numbers have declined ... the memory [has faded] of the heroism, suffering and sheer human effort of the extraordinary men on both sides ...' Let us hope that Christina's book brings a new generation of visitors to this neglected area of the Verdun battlefield: those 'extraordinary men' surely deserve to have their endeavours acknowledged by this and future generations.

Nigel Cave
ROSMINI COLLEGE, TAKAPUNA

AUTHOR'S NOTE

In researching the siege of Fort Vaux I have, as far as possible, used only first-hand accounts of the events that took place during those five days. That limits the number of sources available but has the advantage of ensuring that each one is as accurate as human memory can make it. There is no war diary for the garrison company during the siege, and the archives in the command post were destroyed before the surrender, so the main eyewitness accounts of events inside Fort Vaux between 2 June and 7 June 1916 are *Le Drame du Fort de Vaux* by Major Raynal and *Avec les Honneurs de la Guerre, Souvenirs du Fort de Vaux,* by P.-A. Roy. Roy, a lieutenant with the 101st Infantry who was detached to take command of a platoon of sappers from 17/51T Company, 2nd Engineers, arrived at Fort Vaux on 22 May, twenty-four hours before Raynal. As commander of the sappers he was at the forefront of Raynal's defensive arrangements and took part in the meetings held in the command post during those eventful days.

Roy's work is a treasure trove of wonderful detail. He was a careful observer of the scene and writes lucidly of what he knows personally. He has no political axe to grind, as Raynal occasionally has. His accounts of the German assaults on the barricades match the corresponding German accounts in every case but one, and without his detailed fort plan and his description of the site of each barricade I would not have been able to follow the events as they unfolded day by day. I have also followed Roy's account of how Raynal's letter of surrender was communicated to the Germans. It differs from that to be found in certain other works but it was Roy who ordered the barricades to be opened to let the envoys through and he who remained there waiting for them to return, watching the dawn light grow and smelling the cool, damp air as it wafted in.

The first German officer to enter Fort Vaux, Lieutenant Werner Müller, 53rd Infantry, also left an account of the envoys' arrival, which a detailed knowledge of the fort and a careful comparison of Roy's and Müller's statements have allowed me to reconstruct. They differ on the question of whether or not Müller saluted the defenders, with Roy describing his salute in detail and Müller mentioning only the salutes given by the NCOs behind him. Again, I have stuck to Roy's account. It seems to me that a nervous German officer arriving in such astonishing circumstances in the main corridor of a French fort to find it crammed with men who snapped to attention at his appearance would automatically salute in return, but Müller may not have wanted it to be known that he did.

Having said that, questions arise that no amount of careful study can resolve. To take just a few examples: Roy watched two French envoys carrying one flag slip out of the barracks in the early hours of 7 June but Lieutenant Müller mentions three men and two flags. No amount of research has produced the name of the third man. Did anyone really escape from Fort Vaux on the evening of 5 June? Did Müller speak French? As only three pigeon messages are recorded, what happened to the fourth bird? Were the superfluous men required to serve on the barricades or was it only the garrison who took their turn there? And the most puzzling question of all: what prevented Raynal from ordering the superfluous men out of the fort when he took command on 24 May?

Whatever the answers to these questions, the fact remains that from 2 June to 7 June 1916 Fort Vaux was defended by Major Raynal and his men to the very best of their ability. Cut off from the rest of the battle and forced, like a ship adrift, to rely on its own resources, Fort Vaux held out until it became clear that there was absolutely no hope of rescue. Only then did Raynal surrender and the honours of war were accorded to the garrison. The siege, with its tales of desperate underground fighting in narrow tunnels, the gradual enemy advance, the hopeful messages flashed out into the darkness, the last pigeon message on which so many lives depended, and the agony of thirst, quickly caught the imagination of the world and still sends shivers down the spine.

Here, in the empty silence of Fort Vaux, these experiences remain, and with them the memory of the men on both sides who found themselves involved in events they would surely not have chosen but who accepted the task and carried it to the end.

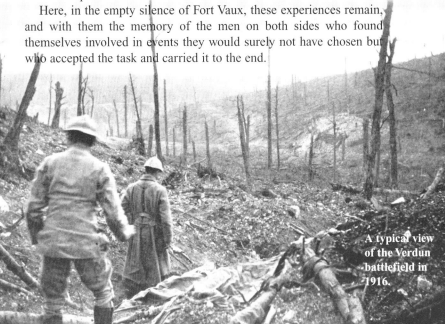

A typical view of the Verdun battlefield in 1916.

INTRODUCTION

It was bright and sunny on 7 June 1916 when the French garrison of Fort Vaux, a battered concrete-covered block surrounded by a sea of mud some eight kilometres from the French city of Verdun, made their exhausted way into German captivity. The German siege of the fort had taken five days and while that was not a long time in itself, its capture had only come after more than three months of increasingly desperate efforts – one hundred and one days of repeated attacks and raging bombardment that blasted woodland, smashed houses, covered the ground with corpses and turned the area of attack into a hopeless wilderness of mud, debris and despair.

Today, the road that leads to Fort Vaux passes through dense forest. With Fort Vaux out of sight from whichever angle a visitor approaches, it is possible to arrive at the car park without having gained any idea of its importance during the Battle of Verdun, or even of why a fort was built there in the first place. It is only when the visitor climbs to the top of the fort and sees its dominating position that the significance of the site starts to become clear. Even then the forest hides the other elements of the complex, interlocking, defensive system – forts, batteries, fieldworks, entrenchments – with which Fort Vaux was linked and which together made Verdun the strongest fortress city in France before the First World War.

Fort Vaux was just one part of the Verdun system, one fort among many, and the smallest of them all. However, its significance was much greater than its size, as the Germans found out within days of the start of the Battle of Verdun on 21 February 1916. This German operation, which was launched with the aim of breaking the stalemate on the Western Front and bringing the First World War to an end in 1916, involved an assault on the Right (east) Bank of the River Meuse by three army corps backed by over one thousand guns. The Right Bank was made up of a series of heavily defended ridges separated by deep marshy valleys. The two highest ridges were the site of numerous mutually supporting defences, each of which would have to be taken if the Germans were to advance.

At first the German operation was successful and there was jubilation on 25 February 1916 when a small party of German soldiers managed to capture Fort Douaumont. This was the most important of the Verdun forts and its capture was a shattering blow to the French. However, as the weeks passed it became clear that far from giving the

Germans an advantage, their seizure of Fort Douaumont had locked them into a situation from which there was no escape. Situated at the highest point on the Right Bank with views stretching deep into French lines, possession of Fort Douaumont was vital to the continuing German operation at Verdun. To hold it, they had to push the lines away. To push the lines away they had first to take Fort Vaux, which controlled their left flank. Their first attempt in March 1916 was a failure and, until the Germans captured it three months later, there was stalemate on the Right Bank of the Meuse.

Who can say what would have happened at Verdun if the Germans had seized Fort Vaux in March 1916? At the time the French were still reeling from the surprise capture of Fort Douaumont. They would have found it difficult to recover from the loss of another major fort just a few days later, while the Germans, boosted by their success, could have pushed on towards Verdun using the two forts as protected bases for further operations. As it was, the three months

Kaiser William II, head of the German armed forces.
Taylor Library

needed to gain control of Fort Vaux took a terrible toll on the Germans and during the summer of 1916 the effort of holding it weakened them severely and helped to undermine their Verdun operation.

Small, battered and disarmed, Fort Vaux was not simply the key to the Right Bank; it was the key to the Battle of Verdun as a whole. Moreover, it remained important long after the battle came to an end, for when French military engineers saw how well Fort Vaux had withstood the monstrous artillery bombardment that characterized the Battle of Verdun, they began to think in terms of building more forts to prevent Germany from ever again invading France from the east. The result was the Maginot Line, the greatest of all the pre-Second World War fortification systems. However, it was not only in France that new forts were built. The resistance of the French forts during the Battle of Verdun was widely noted. As a result, most European countries were busy building fortified defensive systems between the end of the First World War and 1940.

But the soldiers of 1916 knew none of that. To them, Fort Vaux was simply one objective in the awful battle that came to be known as 'the Mill on the Meuse'. For French and Germans alike – soldiers, supply parties, stretcher-bearers, liaison officers, gunners and anyone else whose duties took him to the front in the Vaux sector during the summer of 1916 – there could be absolutely no doubt that one of the slowly turning grindstones of that terrible mill was Fort Vaux.

Verdun in the context of the Western Front.

ADVICE TO TOURERS

Getting to Verdun: Verdun lies roughly 450 kilometres southeast of Calais and can easily be reached by car via the A26 and A4. There are also two possible train services into the city: the three-hour journey via Chalons-en-Champagne, which requires a change of train, or the fifty-nine minute high speed (TGV) service. Both services leave from the Gare de l'Est, Paris. The high speed train stops at the new Meuse TGV station, which is twenty-two kilometres south of Verdun and is connected to the city centre by shuttle bus.

Getting to the battlefield: The battlefield lies some distance from the city. At the time of writing there are plans for a summer tourist bus to run between the city and the main sites but during the recent season the itinerary did not include Fort Vaux, so visitors wishing to visit the fort, and also the outlying sites mentioned in this book, would need a car or bike. As car hire possibilities in Verdun are limited, travellers should consider hiring in one of the larger centres such as Rheims or Metz. Information about bike hire and walking routes is available from the two tourist offices in Verdun. See the **Useful Addresses** section at the back of this book for contact details.

Accommodation: The city offers accommodation ranging from three star hotels to self-catering cottages, bed and breakfast and camp sites. As car parking in the centre of Verdun is fairly expensive, an out-of-town hotel may be a more attractive option. For a full list of accommodation contact either of the tourist offices above or check this website: http://www.verdun-tourisme.com/www-sommaire_hotels-785-UK-FAMILLE.html.

Books and maps: For getting around in the general area there are several possibilities, such as Michelin No. 307 Local (*Meurthe-et-Moselle, Meuse, Moselle*), or IGN (Orange Series) Meuse 55. For a close study of the battlefield itself the best maps are:

[1] the special battlefield map, IGN 3112 ET, named *Forêts de Verdun et du Mort-Homme; Champ de Bataille de Verdun*. This 1/25,000 map is produced by the *Office National des Forêts;*

[2] IGN 1/25,000 Blue Series 3112 *Est* and 3212 *Ouest*.

All three are available in Verdun at the *Librairie Ducher* (the bookshop in the main shopping street). It is also possible to buy IGN maps from their website on http://www.ign.fr or from outlets such as Stanfords, London.

French war diaries: These may be consulted on the website named *Mémoire des Hommes* of the *Ministère de la Défense* through this link: http://www.memoiredeshommes.sga.defense.gouv.fr/jmo/cdc.html. The diaries are a wonderful source of information and clear up many myths and misunderstandings about the battle but researchers should be warned that many are handwritten. The War Diaries of individual forts are to be found under *Région Fortifiée de Verdun.* Fort Vaux is not among them.

Clothing/footwear: Verdun can be very wet and forest paths are likely to be muddy all year, so bring a rainproof jacket and wear stout footwear. As the fort is cool and damp, plan on carrying a sweater or jacket even on a hot day. Make sure your tetanus jab is up to date and that you are properly covered for medical insurance. In summer, bring sun cream and plenty of mosquito repellent, including mosquito spray for your room.

Refreshments: There are a number of authorized picnic sites and the *Abri des Pélérins* café/restaurant, which is near the Ossuary, offers sandwiches, meals and drinks throughout the day. The *Abri* is open from February to mid-November but is likely to be closed on Mondays out of season. When closed, the nearest refreshment possibilities are in Verdun or Bras-sur-Meuse, so carry a snack and plenty of water.

Toilet facilities: There are toilets behind the Ossuary, in Fleury Memorial Museum and at the *Abri des Pélérins* but they are only accessible during opening hours. There are no toilet facilities in the forts.

Access for visitors with limited mobility: The battlefield sites are not well equipped to deal with visitors with limited mobility. The Ossuary has ramps for the main entrance but visiting the lower floor involves steps either inside or outside. The Memorial also has a ramp at the main entrance but stairs between the floors mean that wheelchair visitors would have to ask for the doors between the car park and the lower floor to be opened specially. While this can be done, it involves going outside again. Most of the interior of Fort Vaux can be visited in a wheelchair, although touring the superstructure would be impossible. Visiting Fort Douaumont involves a steep ramp from the car park to the entrance and while the ground floor is mostly level, there is no way of getting to the lower floor without negotiating fairly steep stairs. The

Abri des Pélérins café/restaurant always has ramps available and in fine weather it is possible to eat outside.

When to travel: Although summer is likely to bring the best weather, the thick forest makes it difficult to get a feel for the terrain and the mosquitoes are a nuisance. Autumn and early spring are better, particularly the latter, as by then the organized hunting season is over (hunts can temporarily block access to large areas, including the main historical sites).

Winter weather: Particular care should be exercised in snow and icy weather, as the roads across the battlefield are unlikely to be cleared, salted or gritted. This also applies to minor roads taken by Tour No. 4.

A note on time: Any specific time mentioned in this book is French time. In June 1916 there was a two-hour difference between French and German time.

Warning: Most of the battlefield of Verdun is national forest and, while walking and cycling are encouraged, visitors should stick to the paths and trails and stay away from the edges of holes. **Collecting 'souvenirs', digging and using metal detectors are absolutely prohibited and subject to heavy fines. Forts, shelters, dugouts and other positions are dangerous and should not be entered. Live ammunition, shells, grenades and mortar bombs should not be touched under any circumstances.**

Separate sections at the end of this book contain information on guidebooks, other places of interest and useful addresses. Walks and car tours are described separately.

LIST OF MAPS AND PLANS

1   Verdun in the context of the Western Front..........................12

2   Principal forts and fieldworks around Verdun in 1916 17

3   Plan of Fort Vaux 25

4   The surroundings of Fort Vaux...44

5   The German assault on Fort Vaux on 2 June, also showing the German lines on 8 June and 24 October 1916.............................58

6   Fort Vaux – Eastern Tunnel 72

7   Fort Vaux – Western Tunnel 73

8   The ditch and superstructure of Fort Vaux 133

9   Armoured Observation Post..146

10 75mm Gun Turret..147

11 A walk in the Vaux sector 163

12 A driving tour around French rear areas.................................176

French staff officers at work.

Chapter One

A TRAPEZIUM OF MODEST SIZE

In a comparative table of military events the German siege of Fort Vaux in June 1916 during the Battle of Verdun might not rank very highly. It lasted for only five days, did not – unlike earlier sieges in history – end in a general massacre, and the fort's capture was not a decisive turning point in the battle. For all that, the assault by units of the German 50th Infantry Division and the desperate resistance of a French garrison cut off from the rest of the battle inside a labyrinth of dark, stinking and overcrowded rooms and tunnels, constantly building and repairing barricades, attacked by hand grenades, smoke and flamethrowers, unable to communicate with the outside world and ultimately driven to surrender by thirst, quickly caught the imagination of visitors from all over the world. Not only that, but it helped to influence French military thinking for twenty years after the First World War.

Fort Vaux was only one of the forts involved in the Battle of Verdun. In 1914 the city that gave its name to the battle was surrounded by a double ring of modern, heavily armed forts and fieldworks that stood

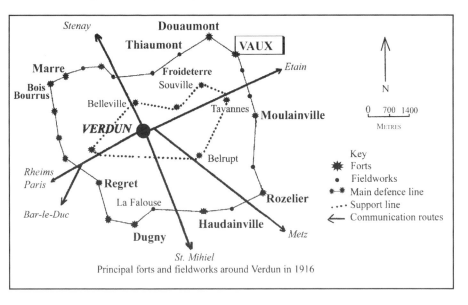

Principal forts and fieldworks around Verdun in 1916

17

The St Paul gate at Verdun. The city walls on either side of the gate were demolished after the First World War. *Tom Gudmestad*

on the high ridges surrounding the city and buttressed its traditional position as a rampart against invasion. This is a role that Verdun owes to geography, for it stands where the east–west road from Paris to Germany crosses the valley of the northward-flowing River Meuse. The city is surrounded by flat-topped hills that rise to 390 metres above sea level and provide extensive views in all directions. Over the ages the winding course of the river has cut into the hills on both sides of the valley, leaving interlocking spurs that project out from the valley floor, dominating passage from either north or south and protecting the river crossings. Streams have sliced the hills into deep ravines that concentrate communication routes into a few gateways and offer scores of concealed positions for observation and defence. The natural strength of the position was recognised from early times and rulers from the Celts to Louis XIV have sought to improve on nature by surrounding the city with the most modern fortifications of the day.

Until 1871 Verdun was not in the front line of defence against invasion by the traditional enemy, Germany, and there was no need to modernize the urban defences designed in the seventeenth century by Louis XIV's famous military engineer, Vauban. However, that position was dramatically changed by the defeat of France in the Franco-Prussian War of 1870–71. Under the terms of the subsequent peace treaty, Germany annexed a substantial part of eastern France and this brought the Franco-German border very close to Verdun. With only its seventeenth-century walls and citadel to defend it from the growing power of Germany, new defences were urgently required and the ideas adopted were those of General Raymond Séré de Rivières, a military engineer with recent experience of modern fortress building. He proposed that new forts should be built on both sides of the River Meuse using commanding heights that were sufficiently far from Verdun to protect it from bombardment. Those on the Right (east) Bank of the river would dominate passage along the Meuse valley and control road and rail communications towards the German border. Those on the Left (west) Bank would control the road to Paris, which was the main line of communication and retreat available to the French. Construction of the first forts began in 1875 but it was some years before work began on a new structure that came to be known as Fort Vaux.

1881–85, construction of Fort Vaux

The site chosen for this new addition to the system was a promontory standing at 345 metres above sea level roughly eight kilometres northeast of Verdun at a point where the hills drop steeply to the plain below. This plain, which was poorly drained, dotted with small lakes and crossed by few all-weather roads, stretched eastwards for approximately forty kilometres, and with the Franco-German border

The ditch at Fort Belleville, built in 1875, with a caponier on the left.
Author's collection

only twenty-five kilometres from Verdun, the military importance of the site for observation and defence was immediately clear. As early as 1874 a plan had been drawn up for a light fortification to be built there that would act as an 'alarm bell' in case of hostile action but the site was too important to remain undeveloped and in 1881 work began on a small fort that would cover the approaches to Verdun from the north and east. Building continued for four years and resulted in a trapezium-shaped fort of modest size comprising ammunition depots, gun batteries, shelters for the gunners and a barracks. Built of limestone blocks and protected by a thick layer of earth, the barracks offered accommodation for the garrison of 298 officers and men, as well as kitchens, latrines, storerooms, a pharmacy and a bakery. Two underground cisterns provided the water supply. The guns – eight in the fort and two outside – were mounted in the open air. The whole structure, which measured roughly 150 metres from north to south and 200 metres from east to west, was surrounded by a deep dry ditch that was protected by small loopholed bastions known as caponiers.

However, even while Fort Vaux was under construction, developments in artillery and explosives were rendering traditional

The underground entrance to Fort Vaux constructed in 1889.
Author's collection

A view of the massive concrete layer poured on the barracks.
Author's collection

stone-built forts obsolete. First, the air-burst shrapnel shell developed in 1880 made life extremely dangerous for unprotected guns and their crews; secondly, the time fuse, which appeared in 1883, allowed a shell to penetrate into the body of a fort before exploding. Other developments included the invention of melinite (a high explosive of much greater power than the black powder previously used) and also improvements in the design of guns and shells that led to increased range and velocity, larger calibres, improved rates of fire and greater accuracy. The increased destructive power of the shells when fired from the new guns and howitzers was devastating to earth-covered forts such as Fort Vaux and new ideas had to be found to protect them.

As a first step the guns were moved out of the forts and placed in the intervals between them, where they were covered by flanking fire from either side. However, protecting the forts themselves was more difficult, as it meant finding a way of strengthening the original construction. Experiments carried out by the French army between 1886 and 1887 showed that at least ten metres of earth would be needed to protect the existing forts from the new high explosive shells, but that concrete was an effective protection for masonry provided that it was laid on a bed of sand and covered with a thick layer of earth. Further experiments resulted in the development of *béton spécial*, or 'special concrete', which was composed of 400 kilos of cement mixed with 0.3 cubic metres of sand and 0.9 cubic metres of aggregate hand-crushed to a size of between forty and seventy millimetres.

1888, Fort Vaux is modernized

In the light of these tests it was decided in 1887 that the new forts and fieldworks at Verdun would have to be modernized. This would be done by adding a protective coat of special concrete to those parts of each one that would be of vital importance in wartime. It was a gigantic task. At Fort Vaux the modernization process began in June 1888 with the transport to Verdun by rail or barge of the sand, cement and aggregate that would be needed – approximately 20,000 tons in all. This was then loaded on to a fleet of horse-drawn carts and moved up to the fort. Water pipes and pumps were installed to bring water to the site. Cement mixers were brought in, hoists erected, arc lamps set up and huts and shelters built to protect men and machines from the weather. To prepare the fort for the concreting process, the earth covering was first removed. Then, for reasons of economy and also to produce a shape that was more easily protected, some of the barrack rooms were demolished and walls were built at each end of the building to retain the tons of earth that would cover it when the modernization process was complete. The barracks were then strengthened with brick arches and concrete supports before being covered with a buffer of sand that was one metre thick. With the preliminary work finished in September, the concreting process could begin.

Trouble on the site

It was then that the trouble began. As it was important to ensure the greatest possible resistance in the concrete, a 'continuous pour' process was used and the site operated round the clock whatever the weather. It had not been possible to find enough local men to work on the site, so an Italian workforce was brought in. In the small villages around the fort the advent of a large number of foreign workers did not go down well and relations between local men and the incomers soon became strained. There were further problems when the Italians, who preferred not to work in bad weather, either did not appear when it rained or simply downed tools and went home, preferring to be paid off rather than to return to the site. To solve the problem the contractor brought in an additional workforce of unemployed men from central France but this only made matters worse. There were constant strikes and interruptions and on several occasions such trouble broke out that the

The barracks at the Ouvrage d'Eix, a fieldwork built in 1888. This is how Fort Vaux's barracks looked before the concrete was added.
Author's collection

gendarmerie had to be called in to restore order. The final straw came in Vaux-devant-Damloup, a small village below the fort, when, during heated negotiations over a work stoppage, one of the Italians shot a French worker dead. With the work by then at a critical phase, the site engineer decided that enough was enough and he paid the Italians off. Soldiers were brought in to finish the job and, seeing that they worked whatever the weather, the French workforce also returned to the site. Calm descended and at last the concreting process could go ahead. This involved covering the sand buffer on the barracks with a layer of special concrete that was two and a half metres deep before burying it under tons of earth.

The modernized barracks comprised the commandant's quarters, accommodation for the garrison, a signalling station, storerooms, magazines, a first aid post and latrines. There were six barrack rooms linked by an internal corridor that ran throughout the building. Each room had two windows for light and ventilation, while a door allowed access to the outside. As these openings were vulnerable to shellfire they were protected by the construction of a loopholed wall which ran along the top of the ditch on the south side of the fort and was high enough to mask them. The gap between this wall and the barracks was known as the 'balcony'. On the north side of the barracks a small courtyard backed on to an earth rampart which provided protection for ammunition magazines. Two underground cisterns with a total capacity of 300 cubic metres (300,000 litres) provided the fort's water supply, which was pumped from springs several kilometres away. Basic sanitary facilities were provided by a small internal latrine block.

Firepower

However, it was not only the barracks that needed protection; the revolution in high explosives and artillery in the 1880s meant that guns also had to be protected if they were to remain operational at all times. At first the guns were left in external batteries but, with the introduction of reinforced concrete in 1897, it became possible to construct shell-proof gun positions in the fort itself. At Fort Vaux this process began in 1904 with the installation, at the highest point of the superstructure, of a retractable steel turret for two short-barrelled 75mm guns which could rotate through 360 degrees, covering all the approaches to the fort. As the gunners inside the turret could not see the target, they were connected by speaking tube to an external observation post protected by a heavy steel dome. Two similar posts on the 'shoulders' of the fort – high points on either side of the 75mm turret – offered increased observation towards the north and east, from which directions it was assumed the enemy would come. Two years later further firepower was added by the construction of two reinforced concrete bunkers known, after the place where they were first tested, as Bourges Casemates. Embedded deep in the earth massif that covered the barracks and roofed with a layer of reinforced concrete almost two metres thick, each bunker mounted two quick-firing 75mm field guns with a range sufficient to cover a wide area on the fort's

Cupola of a 75mm turret with connected observation post at the Ouvrage de la Falouse. This turret is identical to that constructed at Fort Vaux.
Author's collection

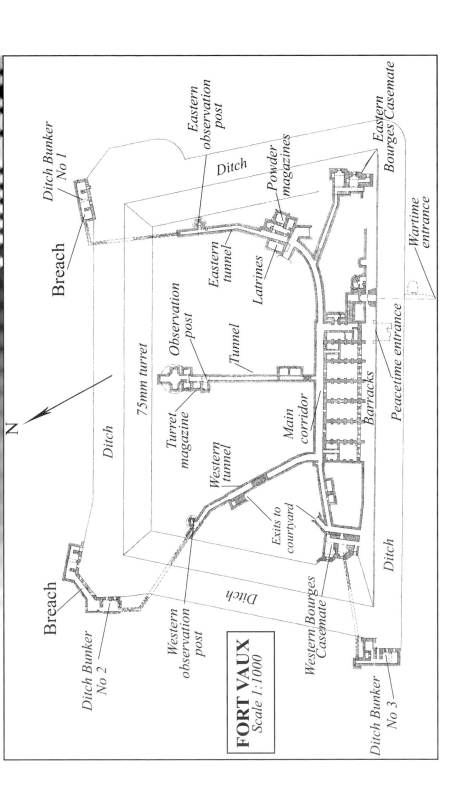

FORT VAUX
Scale 1:1000

N

Breach

Ditch Bunker No 1

Breach

Ditch Bunker No 2

Eastern observation post

Ditch

Powder magazines

Eastern Bourges Casemate

Eastern tunnel

Latrines

Wartime entrance

75mm turret

Observation post

Tunnel

Turret magazine

Main corridor

Barracks

Peacetime entrance

Western tunnel

Ditch

Exits to courtyard

Western observation post

Ditch

Western Bourges Casemate

Ditch Bunker No 3

The western Bourges Casemate. *Author's collection*

Above: Ditch Bunker No. 3, set well down in the western ditch. *Author's collection*

Left: The entrance to one of the underground ammunition depots at Verdun. *Author's collection*

flanks. (For detailed descriptions of the 75mm turret and the Bourges Casemates, see Tour No. 1.)

Surrounding the barracks and gun positions was by a deep ditch whose vertical walls were revetted with stone on both sides. It was defended by three strong bunkers which, replacing the old caponiers, were embedded in the outer corners of the ditch and faced inwards. Armed with revolver guns and light cannon, these bunkers controlled all sides of the ditch and could sweep with fire any enemy who managed to penetrate that far. Surrounding the fort outside the ditch was a wide glacis – an open slope that offered clear fields of fire in all directions – and a deep belt of wire.

Access to Fort Vaux

The fort was accessed by means of a wagon road that led up the glacis on the south side, crossed a drawbridge over the ditch and passed through a gate in the loopholed wall. This entrance was known as the *Entrée de Paix* or peacetime gate. However, in 1889 a new and more secure entrance was created with the construction of an underground tunnel that entered the fort from outside the ditch on the south side. This was known as the *Entrée de Guerre* or wartime gate. Between 1910 and 1912 all the gun positions, ditch bunkers and observation posts were linked to the barracks by strong underground tunnels so that they could be accessed at all times without going outside.

By 1912 Fort Vaux was complete. Its construction, modernization and armament had required a total of twenty-four years and cost 2,900,000 gold francs. Although the smallest of the Verdun forts, it formed part of the main line of resistance on the Right Bank of the Meuse and, while less heavily armed than some of the bigger works, its six 75mm guns covered both the surrounding forts and fieldworks and a wide area of the plain between Verdun and the German border.

The Verdun sector

As regards the Verdun sector as a whole, thirty years of continuous fortress construction and development meant that when the First World War began, Verdun was protected by no fewer than twenty-eight major forts and fieldworks that stood in a double ring around the city and defended both banks of the river. They were mutually supporting – which meant that an attack on any one of them immediately came under fire from those on either side – and they were supported by a host of secondary installations, including batteries and command posts, strong shelters for infantry and reserves, armoured observation

Miribel barracks, one of the many that housed the Verdun garrison before the First World War but now the only one remaining on the Right Bank of the Meuse. *Author's collection*

posts, concrete entrenchments, ammunition depots, pumping stations and searchlights. Most of the forts and fieldworks were linked by telegraph and telephone and the whole sector was served by an extensive narrow-gauge railway system and a network of strategic roads. With a garrison of 66,000 men, over a thousand guns, hundreds of tons of ammunition and rations for six months, Verdun was by far the strongest fortress city in France and in September 1914 the Germans tried to pinch it out rather than face its guns. Although the attempt was unsuccessful, it left Verdun situated in a wide salient that was open to attack on three sides. It also damaged or destroyed the main French supply lines into Verdun, which meant that within a few weeks of the start of the war, the most important fortress city in France was dependent for reliable supply on a single light railway line and one road. While sufficient for a quiet sector, these could not be expected to meet the needs of a major battle and, with the northern apex of the salient little more than twenty kilometres from the main German supply line on the Western Front, further operations against Verdun could be expected.

However, as the months passed without any major activity there was no pressure to develop additional supply lines. Indeed, for the French High Command, which soon faced serious shortages of men, material and heavy guns, the vast potential of the unused resources of Verdun began to look too tempting to resist.

Chapter Two

TO TAKE FORT VAUX THIS VERY DAY

When the First World War began in August 1914, Fort Vaux's garrison of infantry, gunners, machine gunners and auxiliaries received their most important order: if attacked, they were to hold out at all costs. To make sure that this was understood the military governor of Verdun, General Coutenceau, had the order inscribed in large letters over the entrance: *S'ensevelir sous les ruines du fort plutôt que de se rendre* – 'Die amid the ruins of the fort rather than surrender'.

With Verdun as strong as it was, the need to die amid the ruins probably seemed unlikely. Within days of mobilization the 75mm rotating turret gun fired to disperse German troops massing on the plain to the east but little else happened until February 1915, when Fort Vaux was suddenly shelled by a huge 420mm howitzer in position some ten kilometres to the northeast. To be the target of the giant one-ton projectiles was a terrifying experience. With the barracks rocking

Die amid the ruins of the fort ... The same order inscribed on the barracks of Fort Liouville, another Séré de Rivières fort south of Verdun.
Author's collection

Ditch Bunker No. 1, which covered Fort Vaux's eastern ditch.
Author's collection

A German 420mm howitzer. *Marcus Massing*

The 420mm howitzer that fired on Fort Vaux in February 1915 was one of two that stood in Hingry Wood to the northeast of Verdun. Here is one of the pits, now filled with water. *Author's collection*

and shaking around them, the garrison took refuge in the main corridor, where they endured the terrible pounding with hunched shoulders and gritted teeth. Although safe under the massive concrete carapace, they nevertheless had the feeling that with each explosion the barracks was lifted right out of the ground and dropped back again. While most of the enormous shells fell on soft earth, where they ploughed huge craters but caused little other damage, one smashed into the magazine of the rotating turret and another ripped through the roof of the underground tunnel between the barracks and Ditch Bunker No. 1, filling it with dirt and debris. Although the overall damage was only superficial, it looked sufficiently serious on aerial photos to lead the Germans to believe that Fort Vaux was out of action.

Verdun's status is changed

The French High Command had every reason to be pleased with the resistance of its new forts but the ease with which the German super-heavy howitzers had crushed forts in Belgium and northern France in the first weeks of the war shook its faith in fixed fortifications. The fact that those forts were both older and weaker than the modern concrete-covered works around Verdun did not prevent the High Command from arguing that the power of heavy artillery was now so

General Joffre.
Taylor Library

General Herr. *Tony Noyes*

devastating that forts no longer had any value and, in that case, their resources could be better used elsewhere. Verdun, which had so far been comparatively quiet, retained enormous resources that the French High Command desperately needed on other parts of the front. However, it was a *place forte* – a fortress city – and as such the resources were under the control of a governor who alone had the right to dispose of them. For Verdun's resources to become available to the French High Command, this had to change. Accordingly, by a military decree signed in August 1915, Verdun lost its status as a fortress city and was given an essentially defensive role as part of a wider fortified region. With the change in status, the power to dispose of Verdun's resources passed to the French Commander-in-Chief, General Joffre, who had already begun to strip the heavily armed sector of men, guns, ammunition and supplies. This process now accelerated until, by October 1915, forty-three heavy and eleven field gun batteries, tons of ammunition and two army corps had been sent to other fronts and virtually the only guns remaining were those under the rotating turrets. At the same time army engineers were ordered to prepare for the possible destruction of vital parts of major forts and fieldworks in order to render them useless to the enemy. At Fort Vaux, where the guns had already been removed from both the Bourges Casemates, mine chambers were prepared and enough explosive was brought up to destroy the fort's main entrance, the loopholed wall in front of the barracks, the Bourges Casemates, rotating gun turret and observation posts. Thereafter, the fort was regarded as nothing more than a barracks and stores dump.

It was in vain that the newly appointed commander of the fortified region, General Herr, protested that Verdun was now so weak that a strong enemy action would have every chance of success. He was ignored and by the end of 1915 trench systems were decaying for lack of maintenance, roads and tracks had become swamps, and material and equipment lay rotting in the open air.

This was the place that General Erich von Falkenhayn, the Chief of the German General Staff, chose as the target for an offensive that would bring the First World War to an end in 1916. He believed France to be on the point of military and economic exhaustion and that a further major offensive would persuade her that the war could not be won. With France out of the war, there would be no reason for Britain to go on fighting and Germany would be victorious. Victory had so far eluded the Germans. They had gone to war in August 1914 with a plan that involved swiftly defeating France before turning on Russia and achieving quick victory there. It failed and as stalemate developed the German High Command was forced to accept the idea that the only way to achieve victory was by wearing the enemy down. This concept – which was known as attrition – involved finding an objective that the French High Command would feel obliged to defend at all costs. Having considered the possibilities, General von Falkenhayn decided on Verdun, formerly the most important fortress city in France but now stripped of resources and difficult to supply.

General Erich von Falkenhayn, the Chief of the German General Staff.
H.P. von Müller's Estate

In December 1915 General von Falkenhayn submitted to Kaiser William II, the head of the German armed forces, a proposal for a major operation to be launched at Verdun the following February. The Kaiser accepted the proposal, which involved an assault on the Right (east) Bank of the River Meuse by three corps of the German Fifth Army, backed by over a thousand guns. Preparations got hurriedly under way and on 21 February 1916 German guns roared into action, signalling the start of the longest battle on the Western Front. Driving the shocked and battered French troops back towards the fortress line, the Germans took Fort Douaumont on 25 February and seemed poised to take Verdun. With the strongest and most important fort in the Verdun system in German hands and French casualties running into thousands, the total collapse of the defence on the Right Bank seemed imminent. Disregarding advice from local commanders that only an urgent withdrawal across the Meuse would save the situation, General Joffre decreed that there should be no retreat. At the same time he ordered the entire Second Army, then in reserve, to move to Verdun to take over the defence of the sector. However, faced with the possibility that the Germans would seize vital positions before Second Army could arrive, General Herr ordered that the forts and fieldworks should be prepared for demolition.

Nightmare days

When this order went out on 24 February 1916 the man responsible for the destruction of Fort Vaux was on army business at Bar-le-Duc, an important French garrison town some sixty kilometres south of Verdun. Although everything was done to get him back to the fort as fast as possible, the chaos on the road into Verdun meant that he was delayed and he was replaced by an engineer officer, who arrived at the fort at 3am the following morning. A detachment of the 44th Territorials – a local regiment known in Verdun as the 'terrible torials' – was also sent up to the fort and, braving the intense bombardment, they set to work. However, the next day – 26 February –the bombardment increased and soon further work was impossible. Plunging down with the noise of an express train, huge 420mm shells struck the fort with massive hammer blows. Gaping holes were blown in the ditch walls. On the shoulders of the fort the blast from shells falling on the observation posts tore one of the heavy steel domes right out of its bed and smashed the internal fittings of the other one. The roof of Ditch Bunker No. 2 caved in, deep craters appeared on the glacis and the access tunnel to the rotating turret became blocked when

Ditch Bunker No. 2 in the northwest corner of the ditch. The damage caused by the heavy German shells is clearly visible. *Author's collection*

the roof collapsed. More seriously, the rotating turret itself blew up when the demolition charge already prepared inside it exploded accidentally, destroying the internal workings and tilting the massive steel dome sideways. The turret magazine was also damaged by an internal explosion that occurred when some 815 kilograms of stored explosive blew up, probably as a result of the shelling.

The damage was reported to the sector commander, who immediately sent up the following order: '**Instruct firing officer Fort Vaux destroy fort and withdraw**'. However, by the time the order was received, it was impossible to destroy the fort. During the afternoon of 26 February the explosion of another 420mm shell had blown up the room in which the primers were stored.

Aerial view of Fort Douaumont in 1915.
H.P. von Müller's Estate

With neither explosives nor primers, the firing officer was unable to carry out his orders and he returned to Verdun, leaving Fort Vaux to the fury of the shells. Over the next few days the terrible bombardment continued and for German artillery observers, watching through binoculars as the huge projectiles smashed again and again into the ever-changing outline of the fort there was no doubt that Fort Vaux was ripe for the taking. They soon launched their first assault.

The German need to deal with Fort Vaux: first attempts

It came as no surprise to the French. The Germans' surprise capture of Fort Douaumont had left their lines in a sharp salient and they were now open to attack on three sides. If the Germans were to retain Fort Douaumont, which they were determined to do, their lines had to be pushed further away. Unfortunately, the ridge on which Fort

Douaumont stood was covered by French guns on a number of other ridges, the nearest of which lay a mere three kilometres to the south. This was the site of three forts – Vaux, Tavannes and Souville – which, if re-armed, would form strong centres of resistance. Any further German advance towards Verdun depended on first removing the dangers presented by this nearby ridge, and of these the first to be dealt with was Fort Vaux, which commanded all the ground over which the Germans would have to advance. It also offered clear views over German supply routes as they approached the front.

The order to attack Fort Vaux had actually been received on 26 February when, encouraged by the success of the first few days of the battle, Fifth Army Command had instructed the commander of V Reserve Corps, General von Gündell, to 'take Fort Vaux this very day'. However, to do so meant first taking a number of other positions close to Fort Douaumont which, if they remained in French hands, could threaten the flanks of any assault on the fort. These included Hardaumont, a wooded promontory only two kilometres from Fort Vaux as the crow flies, which was the site of four fieldworks, numerous batteries and extensive trench systems. Although they were strongly defended, the Germans successfully carried these positions, which not only relieved some of the danger to their flanks but also provided

A pre-war postcard view of Vaux-devant-Damloup.
Author's collection

signallers and artillery observers with uninterrupted views over many of the most important French positions on the Right Bank.

With Hardaumont in their hands, the Germans could proceed to attack Fort Vaux but at each attempt they ran into devastating fire and had to retreat. Realizing that the French were recovering from the confusion and chaos of the first few days of the battle, further operations were suspended until reconnaissance parties had established the strength of the French positions. Then, on 2 March, the Germans tried again but despite some small temporary successes, determined French resistance, supported by strong artillery and machine gun fire, soon drove them back to their starting point, once again with substantial losses.

The problem of Bazil Ravine

To German officers peering through their binoculars on Hardaumont ridge, this was very frustrating. They could see Fort Vaux clearly as a small, low-lying outline on the top of the opposite ridge only a short distance away. It looked defenceless. Remembering the effects of their heavy artillery on the Belgian and Russian forts in the early years of the war, the Germans could only believe that Fort Vaux was ripe for the taking. But there was a problem of geography. Between Hardaumont and Fort Vaux lay Bazil Ravine, a narrow, steep-sided valley that ran from east to west and was firmly held by the French. The ravine

presented a mass of potential problems. First, the steep open slopes on either side of the ravine bristled with a multitude of well sited positions from which the French could pour fire into any German attempt to cross it. Secondly, the ravine was cut in two lengthways by the strongly organized embankment of a narrow-gauge railway, a wide stream and the long straggle of barricaded houses that made up the village of Vaux-devant-Damloup. A further obstacle was provided by a substantial pond.

Gaining control of Bazil Ravine was extremely important to the Germans. It would not only improve their chances of mounting a successful assault on Fort Vaux by securing their rear but would also give them access to a number of other valleys that led to the inner fortress line and thus to the heart of the Verdun defensive system. But to take Bazil Ravine they first had to clear the carefully sited positions on each side and it was already clear that this was no easy task.

Believing that the answer lay with their artillery, the Germans tried another tactic and on 7 March, with casualties already carpeting the hillsides, they opened a massive bombardment on the French positions on both sides of the valley. For twenty-four hours the French were pounded by every type and calibre of shell but when the German assault troops moved forward, they immediately ran into trouble. While a large object such as a fort could be successfully targeted, small infantry positions and carefully camouflaged machine gun posts could not, and although the prolonged shelling had caused the defenders acute distress, it did not destroy their resistance. As soon as the Germans appeared, French guns opened up and once more a barrage of fire stopped the German attack.

8-9 March 1916: a mistaken decoration

The task of taking Fort Vaux on 8 March had fallen to the 19th Reserve Infantry, which formed part of the 9th Reserve Division. Unhappy at the lack of success, the divisional commander, General von Guretzky-Cornitz, ordered the 19th to try again under cover of darkness and against all expectations they were successful. The exhausted French had not expected any further assaults that day and had temporarily lowered their guard. With the guns roaring again, the 19th swept down from Hardaumont and reached the eastern end of Vaux village without too much trouble. There they met greater resistance and while some units remained behind to deal with the threat from French troops barricaded in the houses, others waded across the icy stream and set off uphill towards Fort Vaux. Here the massive bombardment had achieved

Almost all that is left of the Ouvrage d'Hardaumont, an important fieldwork captured by German troops on 26 February 1916. Constant heavy shelling has reduced it to shapeless blocks of stone and concrete.
Author's collection

its object and resistance was limited. Taking prisoners as they went, the 19th reached the tangled belt of wire that surrounded the fort and were just beginning to cut a way through when a barrage of their own shells began to fall. The artillery had been ordered to fire to a strict timetable, and in the darkness the observers had not seen the swift German advance. Urgently signal flares were sent up but they were either unseen or ignored and, with the telephone lines broken, runners had to be sent back with the message that the attackers had already reached their objective. With the shells still falling, officers pulled the men back some 150 metres and dug in just below the hilltop. While some men threw themselves down for a rest, others moved forward to have a look at the fort itself. All seemed quiet, although the 6th Reserve Infantry, coming up later in the night to reinforce the flanks, did run into trouble.

However, the next morning was anything but quiet. Realizing that

The barracks and wartime entrance of Fort Vaux in March 1916. *Tony Noyes*

German troops were dangerously near, the French shelled the glacis heavily. Defenders appeared on the ramparts and opened brisk fire which, together with storms of machine gun fire from surrounding positions, broke up a German attempt to rush the ditch. Then the German batteries opened up again. Desperately waving signal flags, the attackers pulled back once more but not before they had been seen by observers on the Douaumont ridge.

To staff officers waiting for news in a fever of impatience, the seizure of Fort Vaux was merely a matter of time and once troops had been seen on the

A German soldier views a shell damaged wood near Verdun. *Taylor Library*

glacis it only needed an ambiguous situation report to persuade them that Fort Vaux was in German hands. So it was that a message on the morning of 9 March from an officer reporting that he had reached Fort Vaux, linked up with the units already in position and was continuing to advance, came to be understood to mean that a second French fort had fallen. The brigade commander expressed doubts but when a call came from an artillery observer who had seen a German flag on the glacis, followed by other reports of Germans with piled arms, swinging their arms to keep warm, all doubts evaporated. The doubtful commander of a field artillery regiment, who could see through binoculars that fighting was still continuing, was sharply ordered to cease fire immediately.

Crown Prince William of Germany, Commander-in-Chief of Fifth Army.
H.P. von Müller's Estate

Triumphantly, General von Guretzky-Cornitz sent the momentous news to corps headquarters, from where it was quickly passed upwards to Kaiser William II. He agreed that Guretzky should be awarded Germany's highest decoration, *Pour le Mérite,* and, underlining the importance of the event, the Commander-in-Chief of Fifth Army – no less a person than Crown Prince William of Germany – took the extraordinary step of immediately driving to Guretzky's command post to make the award himself. But hardly had the Crown Prince left than the real position began to emerge. Appalled and deeply embarrassed, Guretzky hurried forward to find out the truth.

The embarrassment was general. Not only had Guretzky been decorated but an official German communiqué had announced to the army and the world that

After thorough artillery preparation the village and armoured

fort of Vaux, together with numerous adjoining fortified positions, were captured in a glorious night attack by Reserve Infantry Regiments Nos 6 and 19 from Poznan under the leadership of the commander of the Ninth Reserve Division of Infantry, General von Guretzky-Cornitz.

General von Guretzky-Cornitz.

The French flatly denied it and the following day a second German communiqué announced rather ambiguously that, following strong counter-offensives against the new German positions, the enemy had *succeeded in gaining a foothold in Fort Vaux once more*. General von Guretzky-Cornitz kept his decoration.

Alone in front of Fort Vaux, freezing cold and hungry, the men of the 6th and 19th Reserve Infantry regiments made a final, valiant attempt to seize Fort Vaux. It was in vain. By now it was dark. It had been snowing all day and in the moonlight their shadows showed up clearly on the snowy ground. A vigorous French defence from the ramparts supported by a rain of shells broke up the attack and at midnight the exhausted German troops were pulled back to their starting point just below the hilltop. Fort Vaux remained in French hands – for the moment.

Chapter Three

MAJOR RAYNAL TAKES COMMAND

Stalemate: March–June 1916

The Germans might have failed to take Fort Vaux but their actions between 8 and 10 March had given them positions from which future operations could be launched. However, they had suffered heavy losses. Junior commanders were already reporting that it was impossible to get across Bazil Ravine in daylight and from staff officers drawing up casualty lists came worrying reports, not just of death, physical injury or disappearance, but of shock resulting in loss of speech or hearing and total nervous collapse.

Nevertheless, German units were now established in a wide semicircle around the eastern and northern sides of Fort Vaux, just below the crest of the hill and little more than 150 metres from its eastern ditch. Although the new lines were not visible from the fort, they were far from safe. Huddled in shallow trenches on the steepest part of Vaux Hill (the hillside between Bazil Ravine and the fort), the Germans were open to fire from three sides and any movement brought down instant retaliation. Below them were the strongly defended

An aerial view of Fort Vaux and outworks on 2 April 1916. Note the shell explosions. *Marcus Massing*

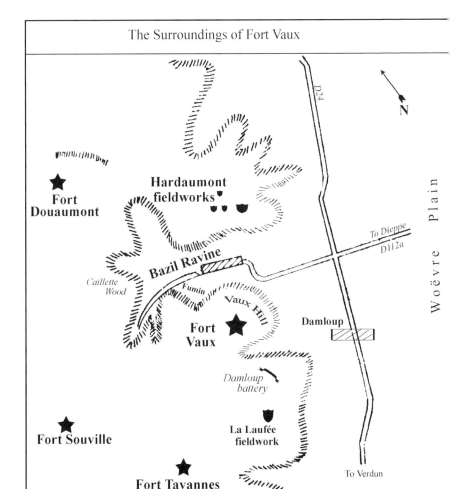

The surroundings of Fort Vaux.

houses in Vaux village, most of which were still in French hands, while the surrounding hillsides held infantry shelters and entrenchments, batteries, a fortified quarry and a multitude of concealed machine gun positions. If the Germans were ever to succeed in taking Fort Vaux, all these positions had first to be cleared and held.

The problem of dealing with exceptionally difficult terrain combined with a carefully designed, interlocking defensive system involved a learning process for the Germans that required several weeks and went to the highest levels of the Fifth Army. It was Crown Prince William himself who insisted on the systematic preparation of any further attempts on the fort. He proposed using artillery to crush French machine gun positions, appointing a commander with a

In a quiet area a German working party takes a break. *Marcus Massing*

technical staff to plan the methodical capture of Fort Vaux and nominating an officer with special responsibility for gradually clearing the French from Vaux village and Bazil Ravine. As a first step, a new assault group was formed under the command of General von Mudra, a military engineer with successful experience in the difficult wooded terrain of the Argonne Forest. Having studied the ground, von Mudra ordered fresh trenches to be dug, communications improved, shelters prepared and guns moved up to Vaux Hill at night to destroy the French positions at close range. The troops did what they could but time and again French artillery undid the work so painfully achieved. For the men, it was pure hell. The German trenches, which were little more than scratches in the ground, were pounded flat each day and there was no shelter. Tools, building materials, food, water and anything else required at the Vaux front had to be carried for miles in the dark through a constant bombardment and much was dropped and lost. The difficulties were so great that men arrived in the front line exhausted; many were wounded before they arrived, others simply disappeared. As for the guns, officers spent days trying to work out a route up Vaux Hill before they gave up, defeated by the shell-torn ground and the vast marshy morass in Bazil Ravine caused by shelling the stream.

Despite all the problems, a new operation was planned for 2 April.

A view of Ditch Bunker No. 2 during the summer of 1916.
H.P. von Müller's Estate

However, at the end of March reports from front line officers were so negative that one of the divisional commanders, General von Bahrfeldt, after wrestling with his conscience, felt obliged to inform the corps commander that his division would be unable to carry out the operation; the weeks of fighting and the terrible conditions at the front had left officers and men exhausted and dispirited. The men were worn out, only four companies were fighting fit and in the general's opinion the operation was bound to fail. When the report went forward, there was consternation. With the planned operation just four days away, the Chief of Staff of the Fifth Army, General Schmidt von Knobelsdorf, called in a senior staff officer and, in the presence of Crown Prince William, questioned him closely about morale and conditions at the front. The officer stuck to his guns and the operation was postponed. General von Bahrfeldt was replaced. Later that month General von Mudra was also replaced, at his own request.

April passed with repeated and unsuccessful attempts to deal with the French positions in and around Bazil Ravine and another attack on Fort Vaux was planned for 7 May. Once again, it was a failure. The flanking fire was so strong that it was impossible to bring German troops into position on Vaux Hill in daylight and at night the French laid a barrage around the fort that broke up the incoming units. In such conditions troops who had not previously served on Vaux Hill stood almost no chance of reaching their positions. Zero hour came with men still trying to find their units and by then it was too late. The Germans had intended to use phosgene gas to knock out the French batteries but so little had been produced that the gunners were hardly affected and from German prisoners of war the French had learned of the coming assault. A barrage of shells roared down on Vaux Hill, flattening the German trenches, pinning down the men as they cowered in shell holes, caving in the dugouts and burying the occupants under piles of smashed wood and earth.

In the late afternoon General Erich von Falkenhayn came to forward corps headquarters to observe the capture of Fort Vaux for himself. Vaux Hill was covered in thick clouds of smoke and nothing could be seen. Once again the operation was called off.

Inside Fort Vaux: reorganization and repair

For the French it was clear that while their artillery had played a major part in retaining Fort Vaux in March, the role of the garrison had also been important. Since the change in Verdun's status in August 1915, forts and fieldworks had been regarded as mere passive shelters rather than as active infantry support points. However, this view was not shared by the new man in charge at Verdun, General Pétain, commander of Second Army, who now took the opportunity to reintegrate them into the active defence of the battlefield. As a first step General Pétain ordered that each of the forts and fieldworks should again be given a permanent garrison and a commandant with full authority over the resources and services available to him. The Bourges Casemates and machine gun turrets should be rearmed and each fort provided with a two-week supply of food, water, fuel and ammunition.

General Pétain also redefined the role of fixed fortifications. If attacked, they were to resist at all costs even if completely surrounded, as this would break the momentum of the assault, oblige the enemy to divert part of his forces to deal with it and facilitate counter-attacks. The new commandants were to ignore events taking place outside but should hold out until food and ammunition were exhausted or the enemy had managed to penetrate the work. It was only when all resistance had become impossible, or when the enemy had succeeded in penetrating the work, that the commandant should order the

General Pétain in the streets of Souilly, March 1916.
Taylor Library

General Pétain's headquarters at Souilly, south of Verdun.
Author's collection

destruction of such parts of the work as were especially mentioned in his orders.

At Fort Vaux repairs were carried out. However, French military engineers sent up to survey the damage to the rotating turret decided that it was irreparable and the turret was abandoned, even though this left the fort without any artillery. The access tunnel was not dug out but the underground tunnels between the barracks and the ditch bunkers were cleared and roughly repaired. The main entrances, which were a constant target for German artillery, were also abandoned and for the next few months men entered the fort through a hole blown in the rear wall of Ditch Bunker No. 1 (in the northeast corner of the ditch) before following the underground tunnel to the barracks.

Fort Vaux, which since August 1915 had been defended by territorial units, soon received a new garrison comprising two infantry companies, two heavy machine gun sections, an administrative officer, a doctor, sappers and signallers. This was too many men for a small fort with very basic sanitary facilities and one of the infantry companies was withdrawn. However, matters did not really improve. For troops living in the open on a battlefield constantly deluged by shells, concrete defences of any sort had a magnetic attraction and as the weeks passed Fort Vaux provided a haven for many men who had no official reason to be there – so many men that when, on 24 May, a new commandant arrived to take over, he found it so crammed with battlefield refugees that it was difficult to reach the command post.

A new commandant takes over

The new man was Major Sylvain-Eugène Raynal, a regular soldier

Major Sylvain-Eugène Raynal, commander of Fort Vaux during the siege.
H.P. von Müller's Estate

aged 49 with a career in colonial regiments who had been wounded three times since the start of the war. When a medical board finally declared him unfit for full military service, Raynal responded to a call for convalescent or retired officers to serve in the Verdun forts and was delighted to be given command of Fort Vaux. Having arrived at Verdun in the company of several other convalescent officers, Raynal spent some days acquiring information about the precise situation at the fort before setting off to take up his post. On 23 May a car took him to Fort Tavannes, where he picked up two guides and, with darkness falling, set off for Fort Vaux. The journey along the main communication trench and over the shell-torn ground was difficult in any circumstances and it was made worse for Raynal by the fact that the serious leg wound he had received some months previously had not completely healed. It was only as dawn was breaking that, tired, sweating and limping heavily, Raynal finally arrived at the northeastern corner of the ditch. Entering Ditch Bunker No. 1 from the rear, he followed the underground tunnel to the barracks and emerged into the main corridor to find it absolutely jammed with men. There was a terrible stench. Struck by both the throng and the awful smell, Raynal pushed his way to the command post, where he reported to the outgoing commandant. When the formalities had been completed, he called his officers together.

Entering, they saw a short, rather stocky man who leant on a stout stick and limped heavily. As they came in, Raynal stood to attention

A postwar view of Fort Tavannes, from where Major Raynal set out for Fort Vaux. *Author's collection*

The entrance to Fort Tavannes today. *Author's collection*

Now shallow and overgrown, Altkirch Trench, the main communication trench between Fort Tavannes and Fort Vaux, still runs through the forest.
Author's collection

and introduced himself formally. At first sight he appeared exhausted but the officers noticed that his eyes were sharp, his questions showed a rapid understanding of the situation and his orders were clear and decisive. The officers made their reports and, with the formalities over, Raynal relaxed and talked about his previous service before setting out to inspect his new command.

What he saw was deeply unsettling. As Raynal immediately reported back to Verdun, three months of daily bombardment had destroyed the infantry positions on top of the fort and filled the ditch with earth and stones that obstructed the view and made defence difficult. There were gaping holes in the ditch bunkers and the underground tunnels. Only one of the Bourges Casemates could be used safely and, although the barracks had resisted well, a massive crack ran along the full length of the main corridor. More worrying still was the armament. With the rotating turret out of action, Fort Vaux was dependent on machine guns, a handful of trench mortars and the light cannon in the ditch bunkers. Observation was limited and communication depended on runners, signal lamps and pigeons, as shelling destroyed the telephone lines as soon as they were laid. To cap it all, the water supply pipes, which had been damaged in the March fighting, had not been repaired. In an attempt to solve the problem, water collection fatigues had been organized in May to bring up water in barrels and cans and according to records in the command post the cisterns now contained a substantial reserve. In theory this was reserved for the garrison but the constant passage of troops through the fort and the frequent rotation of garrisons and commanders had made it difficult to control and no one was sure that the records were correct. As for general living conditions, with the doors and windows blocked up against shelling, primitive sanitation and a fort full of filthy and unwashed men, the air was heavy and foul. Matters were not improved by the lighting – paraffin lamps or candles – which added smoke and fumes to the general stench of dirt, decomposition and excrement that pervaded the whole fort.

It was immediately clear to Raynal that without substantial repair work Fort Vaux might well be unable to resist a determined assault and his report resulted in the arrival of an engineer lieutenant, who confirmed his observations and requests. There were few tools or building materials available in the fort, and the constant bombardment meant that supply parties rarely got through, but there was plenty of debris around that could be used to plug the various gaps and without wasting any time Raynal ordered the necessary repairs to be carried out. The first job was to clear the underground tunnels and restore the passage between the barracks and the ditch. Over the next few days the sappers worked in shifts to dig away the heaps of earth and concrete that had fallen from the roof of the tunnels and then plugged up the holes with wooden beams, sandbags and whatever else came to hand. The yawning gap in the roof of Ditch Bunker No. 2 was plugged in the same way. It was laborious work, difficult to do from the inside under any circumstances but made worse by the constant shelling, which broke up the repairs several times before they were finished.

With the most urgent tasks completed, the sappers set about closing off the other openings through which attackers could get into the barracks from the outside. There were seven in all: two in the tunnel to Ditch Bunker No. 1, one in the tunnel to Ditch Bunker No. 2, two by the western Bourges Casemate and two more blocking the peacetime and wartime entrances. Each opening could be closed by an iron grille but as these would not withstand a determined assault, they had all been strengthened by chicanes – partial barricades that allowed passage in and out. The chicanes were now pulled down and replaced with loopholed sandbag barricades that blocked the openings completely. When finished, the only openings to remain unblocked were the makeshift breaches in the rear of Ditch Bunkers 1 and 2, which, although they faced the enemy, were in constant use by troops entering and leaving the fort.

1 June 1916

On 1 June the Germans tried again to clear their way to Fort Vaux, this time using a fresh division. Watching in the early morning from a cramped observation post on the shoulders of the fort, Raynal could see the streams of grey as the Germans debouched from their positions at Hardaumont in another attempt to clear the Bazil Ravine and remove the danger to German troops as they crossed the valley. Wishing to heaven that he still had the fort's 75mm guns available, Raynal ordered the machine guns in the western Bourges Casemate into action. Although at the limit of their range, the streams of fire from Fort Vaux tore holes in the German ranks, filling the communication trenches with casualties and forcing the Germans to climb out in order to continue their advance. However, they could not prevent the French positions in Bazil Ravine from finally being overrun and Raynal watched helplessly as scores of prisoners were taken. A few wild-eyed survivors from the fighting in the ravine managed to reach the fort and, although they were allowed inside, their arrival made Raynal's heart

A barrack room in Fort Vaux. When Lieutenant Roy arrived at the fort, these rooms were equipped with three-tier beds. *Author's collection*

sink. There were already far too many men in Fort Vaux. In the ditch bunkers and underground tunnels, in the Bourges Casemates and on the stairways, men slumped everywhere, hundreds of them, dirty, half asleep, unoccupied and surrounded by such a terrible jumble of weapons and belongings that it was difficult to get past. Nothing could make them leave. It was obvious to Raynal that the presence of so many unoccupied men only served to increase disorder and make Fort Vaux more difficult to defend but short of simply driving them out he could see no way of dealing with the problem. And here came more tired and filthy men, many of them wounded, who would be another drain on his meagre resources of food and water.

It was now clear that a major assault on Fort Vaux was imminent. Soon Raynal could see German troops organizing the captured positions and digging new trenches. The tireless crews in the western Bourges Casemate kept firing but they could only disrupt the work, not prevent it. As the Germans gradually drew nearer, runners from the French units outside brought news of desperate fighting on the hillside below the fort and a steady flow of shocked and wounded men arrived at the first aid post, which was soon full to overflowing. With nowhere else to go, they sat or lay in the corridor until they could get help. During the day the shelling grew steadily heavier until by evening

Raynal estimated that 1500 to 2000 shells per hour were falling on the fort. Many were of the heaviest calibre and with every hammer blow the barracks rumbled and shook. Inside, men huddled together, waiting for the shell that would bring the roof down and bury them in rubble. The sappers stood ready at all times to dig them out.

Fortunately for Raynal, there was no lack of machine guns. During the day a machine gun company from the 53rd Infantry had taken shelter in Fort Vaux expecting to rejoin their unit in the evening. When that became impossible, the commander asked permission to remain where he was and put his men at Raynal's disposal. Delighted to have reinforcements, Raynal ordered machine guns to be set up in the ditch bunkers, the underground tunnels and at the two main entrances on the south side. More guns covered the main barracks corridor, the barrack rooms and the passage between the barracks and the western Bourges Casemate.

Raynal was everywhere. All day he had moved about the fort, tirelessly checking that his orders were carried out, inspecting repairs, visiting the wounded and talking to the men. Now he could do no more. The repairs were made and the dangerous openings blocked. Anything that could be used to build barricades – stones, blocks of concrete, dismantled beds, planks or picket posts – was piled up in strategic places for use if needed. Every barricade was manned. In the ditch bunkers men stood ready to rush out and defend the glacis while machine gunners and infantry raced to the superstructure to defend the ditch from above. Everyone was armed and prepared. An assault was now inevitable. It was merely a question of waiting.

GARRISON OF FORT VAUX ON 1 JUNE 1916	
Unit	Effectives (approximate)
Infantry	
6 Company, 142nd Infantry Regiment	120
Machine gunners	
Machine gun company, 142nd Infantry Regiment	60
Machine gun company, 53rd Infantry Regiment	150
Gunners	
35th Battery, 5th Foot Artillery Regiment	60
Sappers	
17/51T Company, 2nd Engineers	unknown
25 Company, 2nd Engineers	10
Signallers	
Various, including telegraphists and pigeon handlers	10
Medical personnel	
Various, including stretcher-bearers, nurses	40
Doctors	4

Chapter Four

THE SIEGE BEGINS

2 June

The intention behind the German operation of 1 June had been to clear the French flanking positions in order to prepare for an assault on Fort Vaux four days later. However, with the danger from the flanks already removed, the commander of XV Corps, General von Deimling, changed his mind. Not wishing to give the French time to counter-attack, he decided to bring the operation forward and ordered the assault to begin at 2am the following day. The sudden change caused consternation. A number of the designated assault units were some distance from Vaux Hill and officers had to rush to get their men moving in time. With the heavy guns pounding Fort Vaux and the surrounding area, the attacking troops gathered their gear together and set off for the front in the dark, scrambling into position on Vaux Hill only just in time.

General von Deimling, commander of XV Corps.
Author's collection

The German plan involved a two-pronged assault. While the 1st Battalion, 53rd Infantry, took the eastern shoulder of Fort Vaux and moved down the eastern side, the 1st Battalion, 158th Infantry, would attack the northern and western sides. In addition to the regimental pioneers, whose task was to clear away any obstacles that blocked the infantry advance, they would be accompanied by trained storm pioneers carrying specialised equipment for assaulting armoured positions. However, at zero hour the storm pioneers had not arrived and last-minute confusion in the orders meant that the 53rd moved off alone. As they did so, the German barrage lifted. The nearest German trenches were scarcely 200 metres from the fort and in the darkness they quickly reached the first French positions, taking the defenders by surprise.

For months the French lines in front of Fort Vaux had been smashed by shelling and hurriedly repaired, generally by linking up the shell

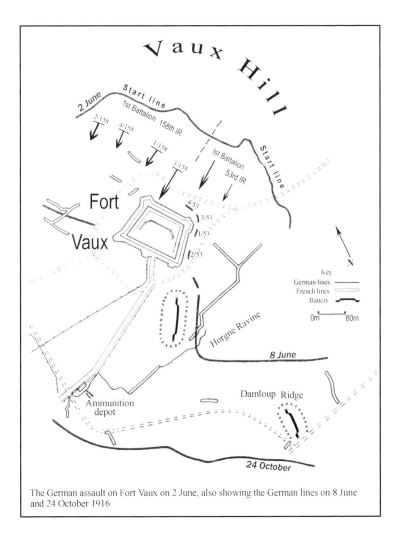

The German assault on Fort Vaux on 2 June, also showing the German lines on 8 June and 24 October 1916

holes. Without shelters or a second position, front line troops simply crouched where they could, withdrawing into the ditch bunkers when shellfire made continued occupation intolerable. Movement during daylight was impossible and it was only at night that food, water and supplies could come up and men could be relieved. When the Germans attacked, these fragile positions were held by units of the 101st and 142nd Infantry Regiments (124th Division, General Tatin commanding). The infantry garrison inside the fort – 6 Company, 142nd Infantry – was in touch with the external units at all times and as soon as the bombardment ceased, they rushed outside, with some men heading for the top of the fort and others pouring through the rear of the ditch bunkers to defend the fort from the glacis. But the Germans got there first and while some of the attackers dealt with the threat from the glacis, others crossed the ditch and scrambled on to the superstructure. Emerging from the ditch bunkers, the French were met by showers of grenades and, seeing that they were already too late, they raced back inside and brought the ditches under heavy fire. This prevented any more Germans from crossing the ditch to join the men who had made it in the first wave. Among those held up outside the ditch was 3 Company, 158th Infantry, led by Lieutenant Rackow, who – still waiting for orders at 2.15am – had been unable to contain his impatience any longer and ordered his men forward.

German postcard commemorating the 53rd Infantry Regiment, the first to reach Fort Vaux on 2 June 1916.

Author's collection

The fight for Ditch Bunker No. 1

When Rackow arrived at the ditch he could see the 53rd cut off on top of the fort. Remembering the failure of the March assault and fearing that this attack also would stall, he immediately ordered his men forward but violent fire from the ditch bunkers drove them back. If the Germans were to be successful this time, the bunkers had to be knocked out before the French could organize a counter-attack. The breach in the rear of Bunker No. 1 was guarded by a machine gun and while some men attacked it with hand grenades, others worked their way round the corner of the ditch and crawled on to the top. Here, they bundled hand grenades together and detonated them outside the gun embrasures, hoping that this would put the bunkers out of action. The plan failed, however, and without the storm pioneers there was little more the attackers could do. But then they had a stroke of luck – the machine gun guarding the breach jammed and immediately a well-aimed hand grenade put gun and gunners out of action. Their place was immediately taken by a tall captain, Georges Tabourot, commander of 7 Company, 142nd Infantry, who leapt into the breach with a bag of

A view of the north ditch, with Bunker No. 1 on the right and Bunker No. 2 just visible at the far end. Sections of the ditch wall can be seen to right and left. *Author's collection*

The same view today. *Author's collection*

hand grenades and held the attackers off until he too was brought down. Tabourot was very popular and when he fell, men rushed to carry him back to the first aid post. Others quickly took his place but the exploding grenades had started a fire in the accumulated rubbish piled up inside the bunker and shortly afterwards a white flag appeared. It was followed, half asphyxiated, by an officer and thirty-two men.

It had taken two hours of hard fighting to gain control of Bunker No. 1 and now that it was safely in German hands and the fire was extinguished, the attackers could relax a little. Exploring inside, they found several machine guns, light cannon and various useful supplies, which they shared out. Sending the prisoners and the machine guns to the rear, Rackow ordered the bunker to be cleared of rubbish and the light cannon to be loaded and tried out. Then he appointed a commander for the bunker and ordered him to defend it against a counter-attack from inside the fort.

The first pigeon message

By this time Raynal had sent out his first pigeon. It carried a message for corps headquarters, where it was received two-and-a-half hours later: *The enemy is all around us; I salute brave Captain Tabourot (142nd IR), very seriously wounded; we are holding on.*

The Germans were pushing forward. After spending some time exploring Bunker No. 1, a small group of volunteers set off down a flight of steps in search of a safe underground passage to Bunker No. 2, which was still holding out against them. Tapping their way down in the dark – difficult under any circumstances but made worse by the piles of planking, discarded clothing, packs and sandbags that littered the steps – they reached an obstacle that blocked their way and felt along it for openings. Finding none, they carefully switched on a torch to find it was a hurriedly built barricade of soldiers' packs, which they dismantled before moving on. Passing under the ditch – the roof was so low here a man of medium height had to bend low to avoid banging his head – the little group climbed another long flight of steps. At the top they could see a pile of filled sandbags and beyond them a stout wooden door that had been jammed across the passage by heavy planks. Realizing that they were not equipped to deal with this, the Germans carried the sandbags down to the bottom of the steps and were just building a breastwork when they heard voices behind the door. The French! As grenades began to fly, exploding in the narrow confines of the tunnel with a terrifying, ear-splitting roar, the Germans dived for cover and sent a message back to ask the pioneers for help.

Ditch Bunker No. 2

The pioneers were busy in the northwest corner of the ditch where Bunker No. 2 was still holding out against them. When the Germans attacked, the defenders rushed out on to the glacis but they were soon forced back into the bunker, where they blocked up the breach in the rear wall and quickly brought the ditches under fire. Unable to approach from either front or rear, Rackow could see that capturing this bunker would require specialized skills. By now the storm pioneers had arrived, but the sudden scramble to get moving meant that they were without their usual equipment and all they had available was hand grenades and small flamethrowers known as *Brandrohr*. These produced a two-metre flame and clouds of thick, black smoke and were specifically designed for smoking out small armoured positions such as ditch bunkers. Disappointed at the lack of specialized equipment, Rackow ordered the pioneer commander, Lieutenant Ruberg, 20th Reserve Pioneer Battalion, to smoke the defenders out.

By now it was full daylight and any German who showed himself immediately came under fire. Bravely ignoring the danger, the pioneers fixed the flamethrowers to long poles and crawled to the edge of the bunker to poke the tubes into the gun embrasures. As thick smoke and flames poured out, the gunners reeled back and the guns fell silent. Seizing the opportunity, Lieutenant Rackow and a handful of other men scrambled across the ditch but the gunners soon began firing again, leaving Rackow separated from his men and only able to communicate with them by hand signals.

Something more was needed. Thinking quickly, the pioneers tried packing sandbags with hand grenades, which they detonated outside the gun embrasures. That was not successful either, but while they were wondering what to try next, the pioneers had a stroke of luck. Outside the ditch a group of men digging in close to the bunker had come across a pile of concrete blocks that struck them as unusual. Under the blocks they found sandbags, and when they pulled them away, a hole appeared! From inside the bunker a hand grabbed a sandbag and tried to block the hole again but it was too late. The Germans tossed in a couple of hand grenades and when there was no response one of the attackers tentatively peered in. It was empty! Quickly scrambling inside, the Germans began to explore.

This bunker was much bigger than No. 1 and it was full of debris.

Lieutenant Ruberg, who commanded the storm pioneers at Fort Vaux on 2 June 1916. *Author's collection*

Sifting through it in search of anything useful, the Germans found packets of chocolate and cigarettes, which they shared out. Then, noticing a flight of steps leading down out of the bunker, some of the men gathered up torches and set off into the darkness. It was a long flight: seventy-five steps before they reached the bottom, then a tunnel under the ditch and another long flight up to the top. There was no sign of the French and, feeling bolder now, the Germans pressed on. They passed the western observation post and continued for a short distance until they reached an iron grille. Ahead of them the tunnel forked, with a door on the right leading to the inner courtyard. A shower of grenades from a hidden position beyond the grille told them that the French were not far ahead and hurriedly the Germans pulled back. Using whatever materials came to hand – of which there were plenty in the tunnel and on the steps – they built a breastwork close to the observation turret and posted sentries.

With Bunker No. 2 in German hands, Lieutenant Ruberg could turn his attention to the wedged door that was still preventing an advance from Bunker No. 1. Creeping back under the ditch with a handful of volunteers, he reached the door and was just attaching a bundle of hand grenades when he heard noises coming from the other side. There was no time to lose! Lacking a long fuse cord, Ruberg bravely made do with the normal hand grenade fuse, even though that only gave him five-and-a-half seconds to get clear. He pulled it and fled back. There was a deafening explosion and splinters flew everywhere, wounding Ruberg and blowing the Germans down the steps. But when they picked themselves up, they could see that the tunnel was open. Coughing and spluttering in the thick smoke and dust, they pushed through the remains of the barricade, passed the entrance to the eastern observation post and were steadily feeling their way forward when the torch suddenly shone on a Frenchman! Shocked to find Germans in the tunnel, he turned and ran and they followed, hurling grenades that exploded with a blinding flash and a thunderous noise. Then, with a shattering roar, a machine gun opened fire ahead of them and this time it was the Germans who ran, dodging round a bend in the tunnel and racing for the steps as bullets thumped into the wall behind them. Stunned and deafened, they raced for the bottom of the steps and threw up a barricade, while at the top the French did the same, blocking access to the observation post and firing in the dark at anything that moved.

Lieutenant Rackow takes command

It was 2pm before the Germans gained control of Bunker No. 2. It had taken them twelve hours to clear the danger to the north ditch and allow the men on the glacis to join their comrades on the fort. When everyone had crossed the ditch, Rackow, as senior officer present, took command. He organized the defence of the superstructure and the two

The iron grille by the fork in the western tunnel in 2010. The Germans approached it from the far side. *Author's collection*

The former military pigeon loft close to the Verdun Citadel, to which Raynal's pigeons returned. *Author's collection*

captured bunkers, and set up a machine gun on top of the fort to control the surrounding area. There was little the defenders could do to prevent this, as the slits in the observation posts were too narrow to allow for rifle or machine gun fire. During the morning a couple of French counter-attacks were launched from nearby positions but they were easily repulsed. There was little French artillery activity – when the Germans attacked, Raynal immediately appealed for artillery support but his rockets went unanswered – and the Germans used the lull to send more troops into the area and dig in. Later in the day two French planes appeared and flew low over the area. One was shot down but the other returned to report and within a short time French guns opened up on German positions on either side of the fort.

At 3pm Raynal sent out a second pigeon with the following message:

The enemy has taken control of Ditch Bunkers 1 and 2. I am continuing the fight in the tunnels. Many refugees and wounded. Officers doing their duty to the utmost and we will fight to the end. Captain Tabourot, 142nd Infantry, met glorious end, wounded defending breach in Bunker No. 1. Request for him Legion of Honour.

Inside the fort

As long as the ditch bunkers were in French hands, Raynal received news from outside but once they had fallen, it was impossible to know what was happening. He knew that the Germans were digging in on the northern and western sides of Fort Vaux but that strong fire from Ditch Bunker No. 3 and from the barricades along the front of the barracks was preventing the units on either side from linking up. On the whole, Raynal was optimistic. With every tunnel transformed into a redoubt that would have to be taken step by step, and the garrison organized into three watches, Raynal was sure that his men would be able to hold out until relieved. Two weeks earlier a French attempt to retake Fort Douaumont had seen French soldiers established for three days on the superstructure of that fort but they had not managed to gain control of the barracks, which remained in German hands throughout. That attempt had taught the French three lessons: that light calibre shelling was needed to clear attackers off the superstructure without damaging the fort, that strong barricades covered by machine gun fire provided

Steps down to the ditch from Ditch Bunker No. 1 in 2010. The passage under the ditch is still so low that a man of medium height would have to bend down. *Author's collection*

an effective means of defence and that hand grenades were also effective when used by a garrison knowing every inch of the fort.

Already conditions in the barracks were extremely difficult. The first aid post was overflowing with wounded, everyone was affected by heat and thirst and Raynal himself was suffering from one of his regular bouts of malaria. With water canteens empty, he ordered the first distribution of water from the cisterns – one litre per man. It was almost undrinkable. The general stench that pervaded the barracks and tunnels seemed to have affected the cisterns and the water smelt putrid. One of the doctors did his best by filtering it through a cloth impregnated with disinfectant but it still tasted foul. Nevertheless, the men drank it avidly. With supply parties unable to get through, there would be no fresh water for the foreseeable future.

It was not only supply parties that could not get through. Late that evening Major Chevassu, the commander of 2nd Battalion, 142nd Infantry, was surprised to see an unknown and heavily laden captain arrive at his command post. Sitting down and wiping the sweat from his face, the new arrival asked for a guide to the fort, explaining that he and Raynal had been appointed as alternate commandants and that it was his turn to take over. Astonished, Chevassu explained that the captain was too late; access to Fort Vaux was blocked by German

Part of the battery in Chenois Wood, where Major Chevassu had his command post. *Author's collection*

machine guns and forward liaison was almost impossible. Surprised to hear that he would not be going further, the captain rested for a while. Then he picked up his packs and returned to Fort Tavannes, missing history by a hair's breadth.

3 June

Fort Vaux was in III Corps sector and when Raynal's first pigeon message came in, the corps commander, General Lebrun, ordered the fort to be relieved immediately. However, at the time the order was issued on 2 June the precise situation at the fort was unclear; the battlefield was in chaos and no one could be sure of where the front lines ran. As General Tatin's division had suffered heavy casualties during the day, fresh troops were made available and at dawn on 3 June the infantry moved forward. However, they were immediately seen by the attackers on the fort, who called down artillery support and, caught in an onslaught of shells, the advancing units retreated with heavy casualties. The first attempt to relieve Fort Vaux had failed.

In the early hours of 3 June a signal lamp at Fort Vaux blinked out the following message to the receiving station at Fort Souville:

> *Situation unchanged. Enemy digging in on the superstructure and around the fort. Request shell fort with light calibre. Large numbers of enemy holding and reinforcing our former front line trenches. Appear to have machine gun in trench to southwest, near south ditch.*

Outside, the Germans were organizing their positions and digging in. The 158th held the superstructure and eastern shoulder of the fort, while the 53rd held the western shoulder and western flank. The top of the fort gave them wide views over the surrounding French positions and while French artillery activity remained light they were reasonably secure. However, during the night there was steady shelling and as dawn broke a French plane circled low over Fort Vaux, followed shortly afterwards by a violent bombardment that smashed the newly dug German positions and forced the men to run for cover in the ditch bunkers. By then the troops that had carried out the original assault were completely exhausted and during the night of 3–4 June they were withdrawn and replaced by units from the 126th Infantry and 39th Fusiliers. The new men had no idea how many defenders there might be inside the fort or what their conditions were like but they were optimistic. When captured, the French garrison of Fort Douaumont – a considerably bigger structure – had proved to be barely seventy men, so the garrison of Fort Vaux might be much smaller. If so, they might

Lieutenant Rackow, second from the left, with Crown Prince William, second from the right, and other recipients of the Order of Pour le Mérite.
Author's collection

not resist for long. Sure of success, the Fusilier commander, Captain Gillhausen, was appointed as fort commandant, while two fusilier companies, together with pioneers and machine gunners, were told off to form the garrison.

While the Germans outside were preparing for their next assault, Raynal was touring the barricades, talking to his men and devising new defences. The western tunnel – which led to Ditch Bunker No. 2 – was particularly vulnerable. The long breach in the roof that the sappers had repaired so carefully a few days before was only a short distance from the barracks and, if it was discovered, the Germans could be in the barracks before the French had time to react. To prevent that, the sappers threw up a chicane close to the junction of the western tunnel and the main barracks' corridor and sentries were posted with orders to resist all attacks.

On the other side of the fort, the eastern tunnel had three barricades – two by the main latrines, where the passage from the inner courtyard crossed the tunnel, and a third just beyond the observation post, which Raynal was determined to retain. With his machine gunners at the barricade by the observation post firing at any noise in the darkness, attacking it was almost impossible for the Germans but they kept on trying and finally, on the evening of 3 June, it collapsed with a thunderous roar. Shocked and deafened, the defenders staggered back, as debris and smoke filled the air. It took them some minutes to pull themselves together and by the time they did, the Germans were already pushing forward. Rapid machine gun fire held them off as, in a wild torrent of noise, the barricade was rebuilt. In the narrow tunnel – not more than two metres high and only one-and-a-half metres wide

In the eastern tunnel, looking towards the entrance to Ditch Bunker No. 1. The chicane wall on the left of the entrance was built after the French retook the fort. The deep hole leads to the tunnel system under the fort. The bunker is inaccessible. *Author's collection*

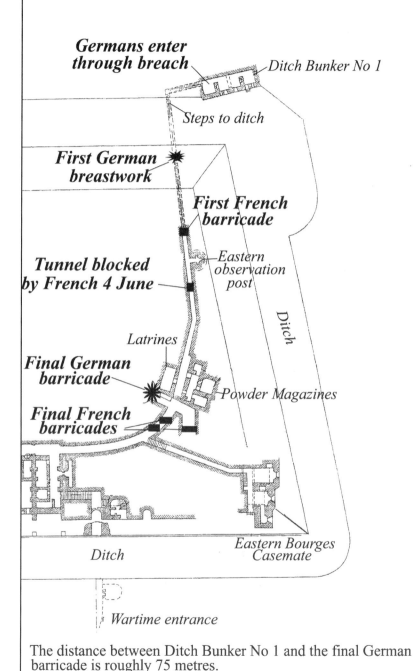

Fort Vaux - Eastern Tunnel

Germans enter through breach

Ditch Bunker No 1

Steps to ditch

First German breastwork

First French barricade

Eastern observation post

Tunnel blocked by French 4 June

Latrines

Ditch

Final German barricade

Powder Magazines

Final French barricades

Eastern Bourges Casemate

Ditch

Wartime entrance

The distance between Ditch Bunker No 1 and the final German barricade is roughly 75 metres.

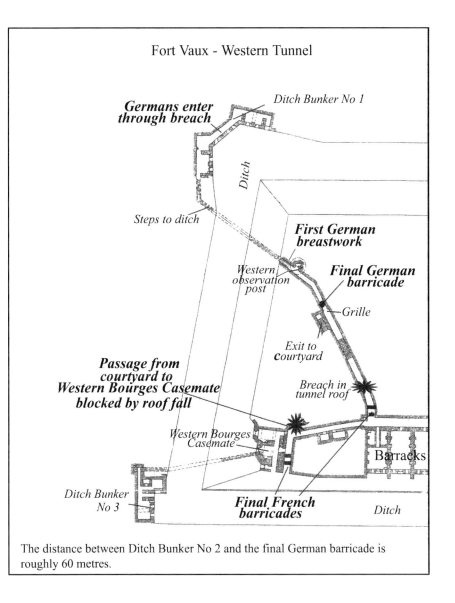

Fort Vaux - Western Tunnel

Ditch Bunker No 1

Germans enter through breach

Ditch

Steps to ditch

First German breastwork

Western observation post

Final German barricade

Grille

Exit to courtyard

Passage from courtyard to Western Bourges Casemate blocked by roof fall

Breach in tunnel roof

Western Bourges Casemate

Barracks

Ditch Bunker No 3

Final French barricades

Ditch

The distance between Ditch Bunker No 2 and the final German barricade is roughly 60 metres.

– the cacophony was both ear-shattering and disorienting, and by the time the barricade was rebuilt everyone was exhausted. There were several casualties on the French side. The wounded were taken to the first aid post, while the dead were laid out in the powder magazine, which formed a temporary mortuary.

It had become a fight between moles. The Germans could bring up fresh troops but Raynal could not. His only hope was that a successful counter-attack would soon relieve them. Until then, all they could do was remain vigilant. Since 1 June no one had slept. With every opening blocked up, even the last of the ventilation ducts in the roof of the main corridor, it was getting hotter by the hour. The air was so thick that lights burned with a tiny flame and from the overflowing latrines a vile stench spread everywhere. But Raynal, doing his rounds of the fort, was proud of his men. Tired, filthy and thirsty they might be, but they stood resolutely at their posts in the darkness, straining their ears for the slightest sound and ready to act immediately. Every man was determined to do his best. If it had to be a fight between moles, there was no doubt that every man would fight as French moles should.

OFFICERS IN FORT VAUX, 2–7 JUNE
Distribution of responsibilities:

Lieutenant Denizet:
Ditch Bunker No. 3 and access tunnel

Lieutenant Bazy:
Western Bourges Casemate; barricades at each end of passage
between Casemate and barracks

Lieutenant Girard:
Barricade in western tunnel

Second Lieutenant Fargues:
Barricades covering the south ditch

Second Lieutenant Albagnac:
Barricades at each end of passage across eastern tunnel; barricade
by eastern observation post

Second Lieutenant Rabatel:
Eastern Bourges Casemate and access tunnel

Lieutenant Roy *(detached from 101st Infantry)*:
In command of the sappers

Lieutenant Alirol*(adjutant to Major Raynal)* :
General surveillance role

Chapter Five

A PROBLEM WITH WATER

4 June

The failure of the attempt to relieve Fort Vaux on 3 June had left
General Lebrun deeply unsatisfied. He immediately ordered General
Tatin to mount another counter-attack as soon as possible, whatever the
cost, and 'led, if necessary, by the general in person'. Once again,
French guns went into action and as dawn was breaking on 4 June four
infantry companies moved off, accompanied by sappers. Although on
the western side of the fort the attackers managed to capture some
ground and take a number of prisoners, the relief attempt failed
completely on the eastern side. With rockets calling for artillery
support, German guns on the superstructure opened up on the

A hand-operated fan of the sort used in Fort Vaux during the siege.
Author's collection

attackers, who took shelter where they could. Once again, no one reached the fort.

Attacked by flamethrowers

For the men inside Fort Vaux, the third day of the siege began with a particularly horrific event: a flamethrower attack on the tunnel barricades. The Germans had been waiting impatiently for the flamethrowers to arrive, trusting to the terrible weapon to overcome the stubborn French defence of the tunnels. Ten flamethrowers had been sent forward but such were the difficulties involved in supplying the Vaux front that four were lost on the way, so it was with six that the pioneers went into action. They managed to reach the barricades unnoticed by the defenders and swiftly aimed the flamethrowers at the embrasures. At once the flames roared out, filling the tunnels with thick, black smoke. Terrified, the defenders reeled back, shouting in fear, deserting the barricades and leaving the machine guns unattended. Blackened and burnt, they stampeded into the main corridor, yelling warnings and looking, in the eyes of one witness, like creatures from another world. As the choking fumes spread back along

The exit from the western tunnel to the inner courtyard in 2010.
Author's collection

the tunnel, panic spread. Men grabbed for their gas masks, gasping and coughing. Many fainted.

Seeing the danger of asphyxiation, Raynal swiftly ordered the fans to be activated. The sandbag barricades were pulled away from the barrack room windows and a great blast of fresh air rushed in, blowing the flames and smoke back into the faces of the attackers. Seizing the opportunity, the defenders raced back to the barricades, hoping desperately to reach them before the Germans did. They were just in time. The Germans were only a few metres away when the French reached the guns and opened fire into the clouds of smoke ahead. As they did so, other men ran to join in, hurling grenades that exploded in the tunnel with crashing reverberations that swept the tunnels clean of attackers. Once again, the Germans had been held off.

The attack had been deeply frightening for them too. The blow-back of flames and smoke had affected the pioneers as much as it had the French, and several of them were severely burned. Despite that, in the western tunnel the operation was successful in

German pioneers with an early flamethrower known as the *Kleine Flammenwerfer* (small flamethrower). The tank held 10 litres of oil; nitrogen gas propelled the mixture 10 metres for a period of 15 seconds. For maximum effect upon the morale of opposing troops the oil was designed to produce a thick black smoke as it burned.

that it enabled the Germans to advance some twenty-five metres. This gave them possession of the exit from the tunnel to the inner courtyard, from where a flight of steps led up to the superstructure. However, matters did not go so well for the Germans in the eastern tunnel, which was littered with old packs, sandbags and other inflammable material. Here, a fire had started. Caught between the fire and exploding hand grenades, the pioneers, some of them badly burned, retreated into the ditch bunker, where they threw up a wall of sandbags to prevent the smoke from escaping. It was some hours before the fire had burnt down enough to allow others to creep forward, this time wearing gas masks.

An attempt to gain control of the eastern Bourges Casemate by similar means was also unsuccessful and efforts by men leaning over the top of the barracks to poke flamethrowers into the windows below ran into machine gun fire from Ditch Bunker No. 3 and had to be abandoned.

Closing off the tunnels

The attack in the eastern tunnel persuaded Raynal that it would be better to abandon the barricade by the observation post, which was both weak and too far from the barracks to be easily defended. Leaving it in place, the sappers closed the iron grille by the observation post and piled stones against it, completely closing off the tunnel. Then, close to the passage leading to the eastern Bourges Casemate, they built a strong sandbag barricade and covered it with a machine gun. Similar steps were taken in the western tunnel, where a sandbag barricade was thrown up behind the chicane built two days before. It was protected by a machine gun that stood just a few metres from the main barracks corridor.

Thus the barracks became the last redoubt. If the Germans broke through, it was there, in the dark, packed corridor and in the barrack rooms, that the final defence of Fort Vaux would take place.

The cisterns are empty!

But no sooner had Raynal dealt with one problem than another presented itself, and this time it was one for which there was no solution. At the end of the previous day Raynal had again ordered water to be drawn from the cisterns but being

The eastern tunnel in 2010: it was up these stairs from the ditch to the observation post that German pioneers carried the flamethrowers on 4 June.
Author's collection

Inside one of the water cisterns in 2010. *Author's collection*

informed that the levels were dropping, he had reduced the ration to three-quarters of a litre per man. Now he ordered another distribution. The sergeant in charge went to draw the water but soon returned, ashen-faced, with the news that the cisterns were empty! Unable to believe his ears, Raynal went to see for himself. Peering down the manhole into the drain tank from which the water was drawn, he could see only mud and a few pools of water. Raynal was stunned. His first thought was that he had been betrayed and that water had been issued contrary to orders but the sergeant assured him that only the correct quantities had been issued. The problem lay in the faulty records left by the previous garrison.

This was appalling news. Raynal's confidence that Fort Vaux could hold out had been based on the belief that the cisterns were full. Without water, they could not last long, whatever the courage and fortitude of his men. Shaken by the prospect before them, Raynal ordered that no water should be issued that day and called his officers together to discuss the new situation. There was no time to waste. Desperate measures were required if the fort was to be saved. As the awful news spread round the garrison, Raynal sent out his last pigeon with an urgent plea for relief:

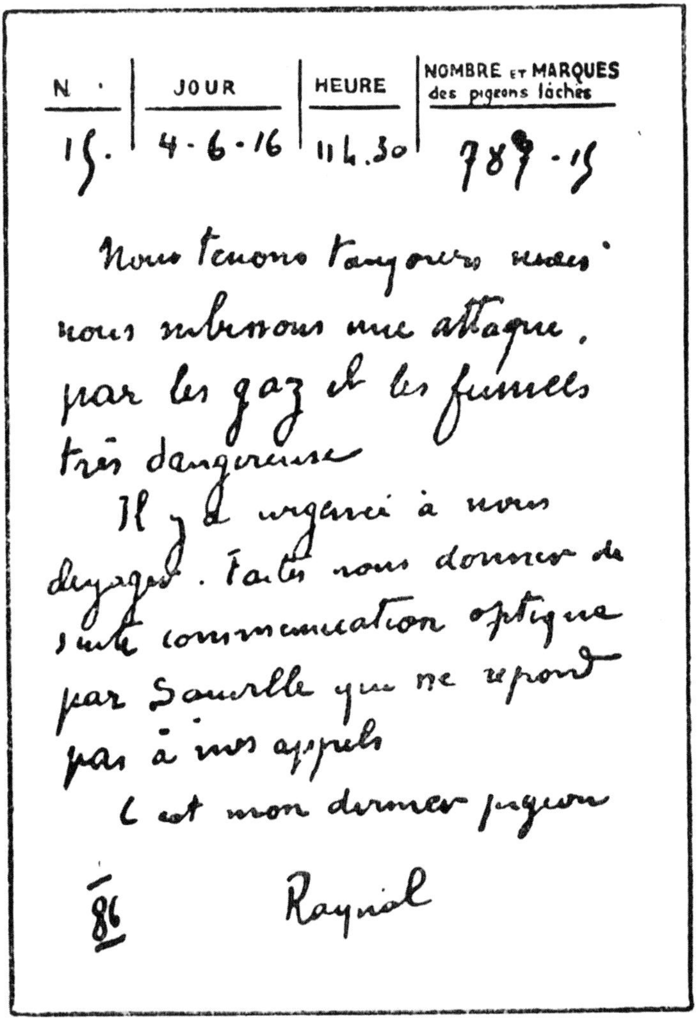

N ·	JOUR	HEURE	NOMBRE ɛᴛ MARQUES des pigeons lâchés
15.	4·6·16	14.30	787·15

Nous tenons toujours mais nous subissons une attaque. par les gaz et les fumées très dangereuse Il y a urgence à nous dégager. Faites nous donner de suite communication optique par Souville qui ne répond pas à nos appels C est mon dernier pigeon

86

Raynal

The desperate handwritten message carried by Raynal's last pigeon.
Author's collection

> *We are still holding on but attacked by deadly gases and smoke. Urgent relief is vital. Request immediate blinker communication with Souville which is not replying to our messages. This is my last pigeon.*

He did not refer to the lack of water in case the pigeon fell into enemy hands. Raynal held his breath as the pigeon handler attached the message to the bird's leg and opened the coop but the air was full of dirt and fumes and to their disappointment the confused bird fluttered back again. As the pigeon was their only means of communication, it was vital that it should fly and taking the bird gently in his hand again, the pigeon handler tossed it vertically into the air. This time it flew around a couple of times before setting off in the direction of Verdun, taking with it Raynal's desperate hope that relief would come quickly. (The pigeon is discussed further in Tour No. 1.)

When he took command of Fort Vaux in May, Raynal was informed that a team of signallers would be sent to the fort with wireless telegraphy equipment but only two men arrived, bringing with them a little black and white dog. The rest of the team had disappeared en route and all the equipment had been lost. Without the telegraph – and now without pigeons – Raynal's only means of communication with the outside world was the blinker lamp. Since 2 June he had flashed out many messages to the receiving station at Fort Souville but so far he had received no reply and, with the situation growing more desperate by the hour, Raynal now selected two of the signallers and asked them to undertake a dangerous mission. Without attracting the attention of the Germans on the superstructure, they were to climb out of Fort Vaux at nightfall, return to divisional headquarters at Fort Tavannes and inform the commander of the situation inside the fort. Then they were to continue to Fort Souville, where they were to set up the lamp in the most favourable place for signalling. The men agreed to undertake the mission and cheerfully assured Raynal that he could rely on them, before settling down to wait for nightfall.

Buffet leaves the fort

But even more desperate measures were needed if the fort was to be saved and the first priority was to reduce the number of superfluous men in the barracks. Refugees from the fighting outside the fort, stretcher-bearers, runners, the wounded and the lost, their number ran into hundreds and they all needed water. If by some miracle another source of water should be found, it would have to be reserved for the wounded and for those who were actually fighting. Ordering that all men who had no reason to be in Fort Vaux should now leave, Raynal first ordered an identity check to be carried out – itself no mean feat in the cramped barracks – and then got the men organized into groups. Their escape was to be led by two men who had expressed the wish to return to their regiments rather than kick their heels inside the fort. One was a stretcher-bearer from the 101st Infantry named Vannier, a pale, slender seminarian who, from the day he pulled off his armband and grabbed a rifle to lead a hesitating section forward, was more of a hero

Fort Souville, April 1916. *Author's collection*

in the regiment than the colonel himself. The other was a 19-year-old officer cadet from the 142nd Infantry named Léon Buffet. In addition to leading his group to safety, Buffet was given a further instruction: he should return to Fort Tavannes, inform the general of the desperate plight of Fort Vaux, and ask for immediate relief.

The only place where an escape might be possible was in the southwestern corner of the barracks. As soon as darkness fell Lieutenant Roy, the commander of the fort's small group of sappers, ordered the sandbags to be pulled away from a window close to the observation post in the western Bourges Casemate. It was through this window that the men – in two groups and numbering more than five hundred – would climb out and make their way to Fort Tavannes. It would not be easy. They would have to drop three or four metres to the 'balcony' of the fort, then work their way quietly into the ditch, cross

it and make off across the glacis. At around 10pm there was a lull in the shelling and the first man climbed up to the window and slipped out. Everyone listened for a German reaction and, when nothing happened, Buffet also climbed through. After a short pause more men climbed out but by then it was too late: the Germans had realized that something was happening. There were shouts, followed by the rattle of a machine gun and a man scrambled back with the news that the others were pinned down in the ditch. Irritated by the failure, Roy waited until the noise had died away completely before trying again. Three more men got out but by now the Germans were on watch and almost immediately firing started again.

The attempt was over. No one else would escape from Fort Vaux. Their only hope was that Buffet would reach Fort Tavannes and deliver his message. Gritting their teeth, the men returned to their posts, hoping against hope for speedy deliverance.

Having watched the escape, Raynal returned to the signalling station, where he flashed out messages at regular intervals, desperately hoping that his two signallers had not perished in their attempt to reach Fort Souville. The hours passed with no reply and he was beginning to give up hope when, straining his eyes in the darkness, he thought he saw a distant light. Could it be Souville? Hardly daring to hope, Raynal flashed out the agreed codes and, after receiving satisfactory replies, sent his first message, describing again the

Fernand Viviès, a French veteran of the siege, aged one hundred. Called up in 1915, M. Viviès and others in his age group had only served one year of their military service when captured at Fort Vaux. They had to serve two more years when they returned to France after the Armistice. *Collection Mme Léa Brix*

desperate plight of the garrison and requesting urgent relief. Souville replied: *Courage, we shall attack soon.*

They would not be abandoned. Raynal was sure of that.

5 June: attacks on the courtyard barricades

Having spent three days trying unsuccessfully to deal with the tunnel barricades, the Germans decided to concentrate their efforts on breaking into the barracks from the inner courtyard; during the night mysterious noises and muffled orders coming from behind the courtyard barricades on both sides of the fort kept the defenders on the alert. Tension was at its height when suddenly part of the barricade that blocked the passage between the courtyard and the western Bourges Casemate collapsed in a roar of noise. Thick clouds of dust swirled back into the barracks. Rushing from his command post to see what the commotion was about, Raynal heard the shouts of officers trying to restore order and found that the sentries, whose nerves had been strained for hours, had panicked and fled, deserting both the barricade and the machine gun that covered it. The Germans had immediately poked flamethrowers through the breach but the powerful air current rushing out of the barracks blew the flames back into their faces and once again they retired, taking their casualties with them.

This was not the first time that a vital barricade had been deserted and Raynal was determined that it should not happen again. He quickly

A view of the inner courtyard. The bushes in the left foreground cover the exit captured by the Germans on 4 June. The long mound on the right covers the barracks. *Author's collection*

proposed that the sergeant on duty at the barricade should be court-martialled and, if found guilty, should be shot. His adjutant, Lieutenant Alirol, who knew the young sergeant well and had always found him to be brave and reliable, took Raynal aside and protested at the idea, explaining the extreme strain which the guards had endured all night. Suddenly, the sergeant himself appeared. Addressing Alirol in a wild torrent of words and gesticulations, he demanded to be allowed to return to the barricade, to rebuild it and take up his post again. Three men, that was all he needed, and he would make it good. Roughly sweeping aside the men standing in his way, the sergeant tore back to the passage, with Alirol racing behind and shouting orders as he ran. Lieutenant Bazy was already at the machine gun, which was roaring and shooting out long needles of flame. Quickly a plan was devised. The sergeant and his three comrades tied cloths over their faces, grabbed hand grenades and then, with the gun firing over their heads as it too was pushed forward, they threw themselves to the floor and slowly crawled back to the barricade. It was only a short distance, ten metres at the most, but to those watching the seconds seemed to stretch to hours. Suddenly, the machine gun stopped firing. The four men had reached the barricade to find that, although the explosion had demolished part of it, the resulting breach was too small to allow the Germans to get through. Leaping to their feet and feverishly snatching everything in sight, they began to block up the breach, while behind them men rushed to pass forward stones, sandbags, chunks of wood, lumps of concrete, anything that could be used to repair and strengthen the damaged barricade. When the sandbags ran out, Raynal ordered the sappers to break up the floor of one of the corridors. Beneath the concrete, which was set aside for future use, the sappers found enough dry, sandy soil to fill several hundred sandbags. These were filled and used to strengthen the barricade, which was almost doubled in depth.

But even while this barricade was being rebuilt, the Germans tried another tactic. From the start of the siege the French had used its embrasures to fire on any Germans who appeared in the courtyard, thus hampering communication with their troops on top of the fort. Having failed to blow up the barricade, the Germans now decided to block it up with stones and earth shovelled down from the superstructure. Raynal was on his way back to the command post when he was alerted to the new tactic and he immediately rushed back to see what was happening. Earlier that day, he had blinked out a series of anguished messages to Fort Souville asking for artillery support and now, with a roar, it arrived. As shells began to fall on the

Looking along the eastern tunnel to the site of the last French barricade. Access to the eastern Bourges Casemate is through the gate on the right.
Author's collection

superstructure, blowing the Germans into the air, the roof of the passage between the courtyard and the western Bourges Casemate fell in, blocking it completely. There would be no more German attempts to get in that way.

Although a similar assault on the courtyard barricade in the eastern tunnel was also unsuccessful, there too the nervous defenders fell back into the barracks in panic, leaving the machine gun unattended. Rushing forward to see what had happened, the officer in charge, Lieutenant Albagnac, was enraged to find that the vital gun – the last line of defence in the eastern tunnel – had been deserted and his nerves snapped. Shouting in fury for the gunner to return, he drew his revolver and threatened to shoot himself rather than be accused of failing in his duty to keep the men at their posts. Raynal sent Alirol to calm him down and a new gunner took over, but with everyone's nerves now stretched to breaking point, Raynal decided to abandon the courtyard barricade and pull his men back behind the machine gun. He did it with a heavy heart. Doing so would not only allow the Germans to enter the eastern tunnel from the courtyard, but would also give them control of the powder magazines and the main latrines, both of which were important for morale. Without the latrines, men would have to relieve themselves in any dark corner, which could only make conditions in the barracks more unpleasant than they already were. But it was almost worse that the men who had died in the fort since 1 June, and whose bodies lay in the magazines, would now be abandoned.

Gradually, calm descended once more. The court-martial was not held and slowly the day wore on. It was a day characterized by Raynal as one of *dreadful physical suffering*. The violent events of the morning had involved the whole garrison and everyone was exhausted. Making his rounds, Raynal saw men coughing and panting in the hot, thick air. Everyone was depressed and silent, crushed by fatigue and strain, and incapable of prolonged effort. Raynal had already noticed that no one ate their rations; their throats were too dry and, without water, the tinned meat was too salty. Raynal himself was not particularly hungry but, like everyone else, he was desperately thirsty. In desperation, he decided to order the last drops of water to be issued. It was muddy and stinking and made scarcely half a cup per man but the troops drank it avidly. However, it was nowhere near sufficient and in an attempt to

The main troop latrines. *Author's collection*

save what was left Raynal ordered more men to leave the fort that night. Returning to the signalling post, he blinked out another desperate message to Fort Souville, calling for the urgent help that was their last hope of survival: *I must be relieved this evening. We need water immediately. I am reaching the end of my strength. Officers and men have done their duty at all times.* As he turned away, a shell exploded just outside the post, smashing the signalling lamp and killing or wounding a number of stretcher-bearers, who congregated in that area. Raynal immediately ordered a spare lamp to be set up, even though he knew it was unlikely to be powerful enough to pierce the thick clouds of smoke and dust that filled the air at all times.

Hope returns

During the evening Lieutenant Roy was walking up and down in the main corridor in an effort to keep awake when he noticed unusual animation in the area through which the men had escaped the previous evening. Going forward to see what was happening, he heard, to his surprise, a low voice coming from outside, speaking French and clearly trying not to attract attention. The wildest rumours swept the

Two veterans of the Battle of Verdun in front of Fort Douaumont. Léon Buffet is on the right. *H.P. von Müller's Estate*

room: it was a French soldier lost in the night, a liaison officer trying to get inside, stretcher-bearers coming to the aid of the wounded or – best of all – a water detail, bringing copious supplies for the parched garrison. The word spread quickly and soon the room was filled with men, all trying to follow the muted appeals. With only one way to find out what was happening, one of the corporals braved the possibility of a German trap and pulled himself up on the sandbags covering the window. Very quietly, he pulled a few of them away. Cool, fresh air wafted in and as it did so the voice outside became clearer. Taking his courage in both hands, the corporal leant out through the opening. There was a murmured conversation, the corporal pushed his arms through the hole, pulled – and suddenly Buffet stood before them, clean, fresh and shaved! The astounded men could hardly believe their eyes. Picking himself up, Buffet brushed the dust off his uniform and told them to watch out for another man, who would not be far behind. Then he set off along the corridor to the command post. Entering, he saluted Raynal and announced in a low voice that he had come from Second Army headquarters.

Throughout the day Raynal had waited in vain for any message or sign that could give him a glimmer of hope. Night had come without a word, leaving him with the feeling that Fort Vaux had been abandoned to its fate. Now, seeing Buffet walk into the command post, Raynal's confidence returned. Telling him to sit down, he waited until Buffet got his breath back and then heard his news.

Buffet's story

After climbing out of the fort, Buffet waited a little while for those who were to follow him, but saw no one. Hearing the noise of men escaping, the Germans opened fire and Buffet, who by that time was some distance away, fell to the ground, where he remained until the noise died away. Then he got up and found his way back to Fort Tavannes, where he reported to General Tatin. From there a car took him to Second Army headquarters at Souilly. In May General Nivelle had taken over from General Pétain as Commander-in-Chief of Second Army, and it was to him that Buffet now reported personally. Surrounded by staff officers, Buffet gave a detailed account of the events at Fort Vaux since the start of the siege. He spared no details but described the full gravity of the situation, particularly the lack of water and the dreadful conditions in the first aid post, and insisted that the fort be relieved immediately. He was then allowed to sleep.

When Buffet woke up, General Nivelle informed him that another relief attempt would be organized and that he would send a man to the fort with the news. Furthermore, for the man who took the message, there would be a prestigious decoration. Knowing that an officer who did not know the battlefield well stood no chance of either reaching Fort Vaux safely or of being admitted, Buffet immediately offered to take the message back, although he made it clear that he did not wish for any decoration. That evening a car took him back to Fort Tavannes, where General Tatin explained the operation planned for the following day. It was too dangerous to carry written messages so Buffet learnt the plan by heart and, as darkness was falling, he got ready to set out. He was not alone. Although Buffet had not known it at the time, about a dozen men had managed to escape from Fort Vaux and one of them, Sergeant Fretté, had also agreed to return. Together they set off, each man carrying a compass, a revolver and a stick. It took several hours of slow stumbling over the shell-torn ground, avoiding the mud-filled shell holes and picking their way round the corpses that strewed the path, before they reached the barrage that the Germans laid around the fort. Here, they separated, with each man taking a different route. Slowly feeling his way forward and searching for anything he recognized, Buffet finally made out a looming shape in the darkness and knew with relief that he had reached Fort Vaux.

At first, the news seemed hopeful. At 2am the following morning green rockets would signal the start of an assault on the southern, eastern and western sides of Fort Vaux by four companies from the 238th and 321st Infantry Regiments. They would be supported by machine gunners and sappers carrying ladders. To ensure the success of the operation, the garrison should be ready to support the attack by a sortie out of the fort. Although initially delighted with the news, Raynal and his officers quickly realized that a relief attempt by only four companies and a machine gun section would be unlikely to succeed. Nevertheless, it had to be tried and they had to help. Assuring Buffet that he would make sure the promised decoration was not forgotten – he duly received the Legion of Honour – Raynal began signalling to Fort Souville.

In order for General Tatin to know that Buffet had returned safely, a message was to be sent ending with the words *Vive la France*. Using the replacement lamp, the signallers hurriedly flashed out the message but the atmosphere was so thick that the anxious watchers at Fort Souville only picked up a few words. Fortunately, they included the final, essential phrase: *… hope that you will intervene before complete exhaustion. Vive la France.*

The entrance to Fort Souville today. *Author's collection*

Following the failed escape attempt of the previous evening, Raynal had ordered the superfluous men to be ready to leave the fort that night. This movement had already begun but, seeing that he would now need every man, Raynal ordered the movement to cease and announced that every man who was not needed on the barricades should be ready to support the coming counter-attack. Together with Lieutenant Alirol, he drew up the arrangements for the night. The men were divided into groups, given a specific exit from the fort and ordered only to demolish the barricades at the very last moment. Observers were posted to watch all the approaches to the fort and give warning of the first appearance of their comrades. Happy to have a reason to hope again, the main corridor in the barracks emptied as the men moved to take up their posts. They checked their equipment, cleaned their rifles, sorted their packs and stuffed haversacks with as many hand grenades as they could carry. Hope even returned to the wounded, although Raynal feared that help might come too late for some of them. There were now more than a hundred wounded men, squashed into the first aid post and nearby barrack rooms.

Another French relief attempt fails

Slowly the hours passed. Soon after midnight there was the sound of increased artillery activity and by 1.30am everyone was in position.

They were in full uniform with fixed bayonets. In the Bourges Casemates and at the barrack room windows observers strained their eyes into the dark, ready to give the alarm at the first sight of a French helmet, while behind them the men stood ready, burning with impatience to race outside and bring an end to their dreadful isolation. At 2am the French guns lifted from the fort and attention was redoubled. In the distance they could hear rifle fire and grenade explosions; machine guns on the superstructure were firing continuously and, from German positions around the fort, red rockets were calling down artillery support. For the men inside Fort Vaux, tension was at its height.

But dawn came with no sign of any French troops and gradually the sound of firing died away. For over an hour they waited, still desperately hoping for action, before finally filtering dejectedly back into the barracks. Raynal was waiting for them, saying little but seeming to lean more heavily on his stick. One by one his officers came up to report but it was no use; he knew as well as they did that it was all over. Fort Vaux could no longer hope for deliverance from outside. They would have to find a solution to their problem on their own.

It was only later that the garrison of Fort Vaux found out what had happened that morning. The attacking units had been met by sustained artillery and grenade fire. This was so heavy that organized forward movement became impossible and it was only in small, uncoordinated groups that the men advanced. As officers fell, including a battalion commander, the remnants began to withdraw but such was the violence of the fire that only a handful managed to return to their starting positions. The carnage did not discourage General Nivelle from immediately ordering another relief attempt to be made two days later.

Calling for the signallers, Raynal blinked out a message but only a few incomprehensible phrases were picked up. Quickly the barricades were rebuilt and, as the openings so hopefully created were closed off, the men fell silent again. Dropping their gear, they found a place to slump down and sank back into the silence and torpor that had reigned before Buffet returned.

The situation outside

For the Germans outside Fort Vaux the day was far from silent. Having failed in their relief attempt, the French ordered their guns into increased action and soon Vaux Hill resembled an erupting volcano. Crashing down on top of the fort, the shells flung up great blocks of

**Captain Gillhausen,
39th Fusiliers.**
Author's collection

concrete that smashed the men's makeshift shelters and filled the air with smoke and dirt. For the Germans, it was like being caught in a hellish firework display. To escape, every man who could do so ran for the ditch bunkers or crammed into the narrow underground tunnels but the smoke and fumes were so great that even here gas masks had to be worn. Rest and sleep were impossible. Candles blew out with every shell that fell, messengers were constantly passing along the tunnels with orders or instructions and everyone had to be ready to dash out at any time and repel an attack. In the early hours of 6 June conditions on Fort Vaux were so terrible that, in one of his reports, Captain Gillhausen described them as unbearable and asked for all units to be immediately relieved. Of the two companies of Fusiliers that had taken up position on 4 June, all that remained were two officers and 119 other ranks; the pioneers had been reduced to twenty-five men and there were only seven machine guns. During the afternoon a heavy shell smashed into Bunker No. 2, burying several men under the rubble and partially blocking up the exit. Panic began to spread and it took all the force of Captain Gillhausen's personality to calm matters down. By now they were expecting another French assault at any moment and Gillhausen ordered that the exit should be cleared to allow men to get out of the bunker quickly when the need arose.

The attack came that evening and once again it was unsuccessful. Even before they moved off, the relieving troops had suffered heavily from German shelling and although a small number of them did manage to reach the western side of the fort, they were quickly driven off.

It was stalemate. The relief parties could not reach the fort, the Germans could not get in and the French could not get out. The Germans still had no idea how many men were inside Fort Vaux and they knew nothing of the water problem or the communication difficulties. For his part, Raynal did not know how many Germans were outside or how difficult their conditions might be but he knew only too well that his men had no water and that unless help came quickly it would be too late.

Chapter Six

SURRENDER

6 June

During the early afternoon of 6 June Raynal and his remaining officers – by now four were wounded, one of them seriously – were meeting in his command post when a ghastly sight appeared in the doorway. A man swathed in bloody bandages from head to hips stood gripping the door jamb and staring at them wildly, his eyes sunken deep in a chalk-white face. Getting up, Raynal gently asked what he wanted. Between lips so swollen that he could hardly speak, the wounded man whispered, *A drink! A drink or I'll kill myself!* Quietly, Raynal got up and fetched a chair. He sat the man down and in fatherly tones asked about his parents, talked about home and family and then, gently, about a soldier's duty. Gradually the anguished man calmed down until, leaning against Raynal like an old friend, he began to cry. Then he got up and slowly left the command post, helped along by the runners who always congregated outside. It was with tears in his eyes that Raynal turned back to his seat.

The man's appearance had shocked Raynal and his officers deeply. Despite the bandages, they could see that the man was very young and his dreadful sufferings reminded them of the plight of everyone in the fort. Doing his rounds later that day Raynal saw discouragement on every face. Men who had previously reacted to his words now looked at him with empty eyes, unable to respond. For three days there had been no water and everywhere men were groaning and begging for it. Moving from barricade to barricade Raynal saw men licking the humidity that streamed down the walls or – as it was raining – tying pieces of cloth to sticks and poking them outside in the hope of catching a drop of the precious moisture, however

The first aid post in Fort Vaux in 2010.
Author's collection

small. Worse, the doctor reported that some men were drinking their own urine, which only made them vomit and left them thirstier than before.

By now conditions in the barracks were difficult in the extreme. It was stiflingly hot but the men had to be fully dressed at all times in case of an alert and many lay on the floor in the hope of finding cooler air to breathe. With the main latrines covered by German machine guns, men relieved themselves where they could and this, coupled with the presence of hundreds of unwashed men, stinking infected wounds and decaying corpses, combined to lower morale to unbearable levels. It was even worse in the first aid post and neighbouring barrack rooms, where scores of men, some severely wounded, had lain for days with unwashed wounds, tossing and burning with fever as infection spread.

Seeing their suffering, Raynal decided that Fort Vaux had done its duty. Cut off from the rest of the battle for five days, they had held their own against troops who could be relieved or reinforced at will. They had fought supremely well but now they had reached the end. Returning to the command post with a step which – Raynal hoped – looked firm and resolute, he blinked out another message, describing again the awful conditions in the fort and emphasizing the courage and determination of all his men. He listed his officers by name, mentioned

A French first aid post somewhere in the Vaux sector, May 1916.
Collection Mme Léa Brix

Aerial view of Fort Vaux before the Battle of Verdun. *Marcus Massing*

The facade of Fort Vaux today. *Author's collection*

The cupola of the 75mm gun turret, blown out by the Germans on 2 November 1916. *Author's collection*

The underground 'wartime entrance' to Fort Vaux, still full of rubble and debris. *Author's collection*

Damage in the western
tunnel under Fort Vaux.
This tunnel leads to
Ditch Bunker No. 2.
Author's collection

The iron grille at the
entrance to Ditch
Bunker No. 2. Just
beyond the grille an
unsecured shaft in the
floor leads to the deep
tunnel system excavated
after the Battle of
Verdun. *Author's collection*

The start of one of the six rock tunnels excavated under Fort Vaux during 1917–18. These provided safe passage between the fort's vital organs and also led to remote access outside the fort. *Author's collection*

The tunnel to the destroyed 75mm turret showing damage to the roof caused by a German 420mm shell on 26 February 1916. The floor has been dug away to allow men to pass the hanging reinforcing bars. *Author's collection*

Under the cupola of an identical 75mm turret at the Ouvrage de la Falouse. The destruction of Fort Vaux's turret is so complete that nothing remains of the original fittings. *Author's collection*

A rusting 75mm field gun limber still standing in the forest more than ninety years after the end of the First World War. *Author's collection*

Like something from outer space: a Pamart Casemate for two machine guns photographed close to Fort St Michel. *Author's collection*

A rusting 75mm gun stands in the inaccessible eastern Bourges Casemate at Fort Vaux. *Author's collection*

A German observation post on a hilltop directly in line with Fort Vaux.
Author's collection

The pit for a German 380mm gun at Duzey, north of Verdun. On 21 February 1916 the gun here fired the first round in the Battle of Verdun.
Author's collection

Part of the facade of Fort Douaumont showing the massive layer of concrete poured on to the original stonework and the damage caused by a huge French 400mm shell in October 1916. *Author's collection*

The Bussière gun turret at Fort Souville. The 155mm gun here was originally raised by steam pressure. *Author's collection*

Water being sterilized with chemicals before being stored. *Taylor Library*

the seven men killed and seventy-six wounded and ended with the same despairing plea he had made before: ... *hope that you will intervene before complete exhaustion.*

With the message sent, Raynal waited hopefully for an answering flash but none came. In any case, it was too late now. The die was cast. It was only a matter of time. He thought that they were abandoned but he was wrong. At 8.30pm that evening General Joffre sent a congratulatory message to the beleaguered defenders of Fort Vaux:

> *The Commander-in-Chief wishes to express to the commandant of the fort, the commander of the garrison company and their men his satisfaction at their magnificent defence against the repeated assaults of the enemy.*

This was followed by another message addressed to Raynal in person: *Major Raynal, 7th Algerian Tirailleurs, is hereby promoted to the rank of Commander of the Legion of Honour.* But neither message was picked up and it was as prisoners of war that the defenders of Fort Vaux learned that, although they had been besieged, they had never been forgotten.

Surrender

It was the end. Once more, Raynal called his officers together, this time with the doors closed. Two of the doctors were also present. He asked each man for his opinion but they could hardly get a word out. Fatigue and discouragement made it impossible to imagine any new type of

A postwar photograph of Major Raynal wearing the Legion of Honour awarded for his defence of Fort Vaux. *Marcus Massing*

action and with mouths and throats so dry, speech was almost impossible. The question of surrender was raised but at first his officers refused to consider the idea. Shut up inside the fort for days without news of the outside world, they imagined France to be depending on them; if they gave way the Germans would surge along the ridge, sweeping resistance aside and threatening Verdun itself. Finally, realizing that they were powerless to influence future events, they nodded their approval and taking up a sheet of paper, Raynal began to write:

Fort Vaux, 7 June 1916.

MAJOR RAYNAL, COMMANDANT OF FORT VAUX, TO THE COMMANDER OF THE GERMAN TROOPS ATTACKING FORT VAUX.

Commander,

I have the honour to inform you that I am disposed to cede to you the premises and various dependent works of the fort that I am defending against you on condition that the honours of war be accorded to the garrison and that those measures be taken which the officer carrying this document will explain to you.

In a ceremony held in Paris, Mme Raynal receives from General Cousin the Legion of Honour awarded to her husband for his defence of the fort, June 1916. *Collection Vieillot*

One of your officers may then attend the fort to carry out reconnaissance and to determine, together with my representative, the terms on which the garrison will leave.

Please accept this expression of my esteem,

RAYNAL

With the letter finished, Raynal handed it round and Lieutenant Bénazet, who had taught German before the war, offered to take it out of the barracks at first light. He would carry a white flag and be accompanied by a bugler. As the state of alert had to be maintained, the men would not be informed immediately but certain preparations could begin, including putting the machine guns out of action and destroying the documents in the command post. There were hundreds of these – reports, sketch maps, orders, plans and communiqués – and with no fire in which to burn them, the documentary archives of Fort Vaux were sorted, bundled up and tossed into the deep cesspits under

French soldiers at R1, an entrenchment close to Fort Vaux. The determined resistance of French troops here helped to prevent the Germans from surrounding the fort during the siege. See Tour No. 3.
Collection Vieillot

the officers' latrines. Then a flag had to be made. This was a problem until one of the officers came up with the idea of using the parachutes from the signal rockets in the ordnance store. They were of pale greyish brown silk – hardly the regulation colour for such a flag but it would do. Having cut the parachutes up, Lieutenant Roy's orderly, who was not used to sewing, was given a needle and thread and told to stitch them together. The result was rather rough but privately Roy thought it the finest flag he had ever seen.

Having attached the flag to a stick and found a bugler, they started to discuss the place of exit. The tunnels from the barracks to the ditch bunkers were completely blocked by massive barriers of stone and concrete. Any attempt to dismantle even a part of them would be likely to alarm the German sentries on the other side, with potentially fatal results for the envoys. An exit directly into the courtyard at the rear of the barracks would be the best but of the two possibilities, one had caved in and the other was already in German hands. That left the passage by the western Bourges Casemate, where it opened to the south. Here the barricades could be opened without attracting unwelcome attention and once the envoys were outside, it was hoped that the white flag and the bugle would protect them.

In the hot, deep gloom of the barracks a heavy silence reigned. With mouths and throats so parched, talking or smoking was impossible and any man who was not on duty slumped on the floor or against the wall, half asleep. They were all completely drained. Since 2 June the garrison had made superhuman efforts; they had borne every privation with courage and good humour and now they waited for the end, leaning against one another in the filthy, debris-filled rooms and corridors, surrounded by their belongings. Even now, Raynal noted, every man had a rifle within reach. From the signalling station messages were sent out repeatedly in the hope that somehow, sometime, an answer would be received. Peering desperately through the sandbagged windows of the barracks, Raynal's officers imagined that they could see more French relief parties heading towards the fort ready to throw themselves on the Germans and relieve the garrison from their dreadful situation. They talked about the reaction in France to the surrender. Would they be understood? What if there had been more pigeons, more water, another means of contacting the rear or of getting help? Could things have been different? And all the time they stared out at the dark shape of Fort Souville, hoping against hope for a flash, a message, an idea that would save them.

Slowly the hours dragged by until it was time to tell the garrison.

The entrance to the western tunnel as seen by the peace envoys.
Author's collection

Raynal stepped out of the command post, each officer assembled his men and the momentous news was given: the fort would surrender! The message spread like wildfire and hope returned as Raynal began his final round. Slowly, with his stick tapping loudly on the floor, he made his way from barricade to barricade, speaking to the men and reminding them to stay calm and alert. He visited the first aid post and told the wounded that their ordeal would soon be over. Then, while the signallers sent out their final message, Raynal thanked his men for the magnificent manner in which they had done their duty, ending with a patriotic cry of '*Vive la France!*' Then he returned to the command post and silence descended once more.

7 June: The envoys leave the barracks

It was just getting light as Lieutenant Roy and a small group of sappers removed enough of the double barricade in the passage by the western Bourges Casemate to allow Lieutenant Bénazet and the bugler, 24-year-old Joseph Coste, to slip out. With stones and debris crunching under their feet, the two men set off, with the bugle blowing loudly and Bénazet shouting *Deutschen soldaten! Schiessen Sie nicht!* (*German soldiers! Don't shoot.*) Waiting tensely at the barricades, Roy stared down the passage at the growing light, smelling the damp air as it wafted in and realizing with wonder that it had been raining.

At the same time in the western tunnel Lieutenant Werner Müller was trying to get some sleep. A machine gunner with the 53rd Infantry, he had been sent forward with his section to support the 39th Fusiliers in their assault on the fort. The action of the previous day had kept him very busy and he was tired, but rocket signals and news of suspicious movements prevented him from

The same entrance seen from the German side.
Author's collection

sleeping. Yearning for a bit of peace, Müller was suddenly startled by the sound of running feet as a sentry raced up to him with the news that he could see a flag! Not knowing what to think, Müller ran forward to find, some ten metres away and – to his amazement – some five metres *behind* the German machine gun position – something that looked like a small white flag. Not knowing the fort well, Müller was unaware that here was an opening that allowed access to the courtyard and his first thought was that an enemy patrol had somehow managed to get into the tunnel and had left the flag there to taunt them. As he moved towards the machine gun to investigate, another flag appeared, this one on a long stick, and with it he saw French soldiers. As he drew his revolver, the leading man shouted *Nicht schiessen!* and, in response to questions, explained that he was carrying a letter for the German commander.

Electrified by the news, Müller told Bénazet to follow him and then raced back along the tunnel to the command post, spreading the word as he went. All fatigue forgotten, he tore up the steps into Bunker No. 2 shouting *Captain, French soldiers are coming*, and handed over the letter. Astonished, Captain Gillhausen read the letter and instructed Müller to return with Bénazet, giving him full powers to negotiate the terms of surrender. Quickly ordering two NCOs to accompany him, Müller followed as Bénazet raced over the top of the fort and dived into a battered opening situated right under the muzzle of a German gun. Scurrying behind – this part of the fort had been the special target of French machine guns and he had no desire to linger – Müller found himself in a dilapidated passage where Lieutenant Roy was waiting. Saluting, Müller introduced himself. Roy saluted in return and asked him to follow. After a few steps they turned into the main corridor of the barracks and Müller's eyes widened.

It was an astonishing sight. Raynal had told his men to get ready to leave and the corridor was lined with row upon row of filthy and unshaven men, uniformed, helmeted and absolutely silent. At Roy's command of *Garde à vous,* they snapped to attention, all eyes riveted on the advancing group. Müller had not expected this and with the NCOs saluting behind him, he marched down the corridor with his right hand rigidly locked in salute and his left hand flattened against the hilt of a short dagger that hung from his belt. To Lieutenant Roy he almost looked as if he was on parade. With their hobnail boots crashing on the floor, the little group swept down the corridor between the massed ranks. They passed the communications room, which was packed with men tensely watching the approaching group, and reached the command post. Here, Roy stepped back, leaving Müller to enter the lion's den alone.

The western tunnel. It was along here that Müller raced with the surrender letter. *Author's collection*

The main corridor in the barracks. Müller and Roy advanced towards the lights at the end. *Author's collecti*

Raynal was waiting. Surrounded by his officers, unwashed and unshaven, he received Müller's salute proudly, saluted in return and introduced himself. There was an exchange of names – to Lieutenant Roy they rang like the clash of swords – and then the discussions began. Stiffly, but with glowing eyes, Müller announced that he had been given full powers to discuss the terms of surrender. Raynal re-read the letter that he had earlier written and, having assured himself that his men would be treated honourably, he turned it over and wrote:

SURRENDER OF FORT VAUX ON THE FOLLOWING TERMS:
Honours of war
Treatment with consideration
Officers to keep their orderlies
Officers and men to keep their personal belongings
I hereby hand the premises and works still under my command in Fort Vaux to German forces.

Fort Vaux, 7 May 1916
The fort commandant,
RAYNAL

Müller read the document and, still appearing unable to believe his good fortune, he signed his agreement. At the time no one noticed that the document was wrongly dated May not June and even if they had, no one would have mentioned it.

With the formalities over, everyone relaxed. Raynal handed over the fort's decorative brass keys and presented Müller with his own map case, while Roy gave Müller his revolver. Realizing that they were all thirsty, Müller handed round his canteen of coffee and everyone took a drink, including Raynal. By now, more German officers had arrived and together with their French counterparts they set off to inspect their new possession. From the Bourges Casemates to the food store, everything was investigated and noted. Visiting the first aid post,

The entrance to the western tunnel, along which the men of the garrison made their way into captivity. *Author's collection*

where eighteen seriously wounded men had lain for days without food or water, Müller assured them that by nightfall they would be receiving medical care. As transporting such seriously injured men out of the fort would require many stretcher-bearers, it was immediately agreed that eighty men would remain behind for the purpose.

While the inspections were taking place, Raynal's men got on with preparing to leave. They piled their arms and ammunition along the walls, keeping only a few personal belongings, including the all-important canteen and cup. By now many more Germans had arrived, all in the highest spirits over the surprising events of the morning and curious to see the fort and its garrison. As they all milled around, a lively exchange began and more than one French soldier lost a button or badge to 'the girl back home'. Müller raised a laugh by taking the collar badge of a French machine gunner whose regimental number was also fifty-three and pinning it on himself. There was more laughter when another Frenchman offered him a piece of chocolate. In return Müller held out his canteen, expecting the man to have a quick drink and hand it back, but the thirsty man just kept on swallowing and it was only when Müller roared 'Stop' at the top of his voice that he meekly returned the canteen to its owner. Seeing that matters could easily get out of hand, Müller snapped out a series of sharp orders that were repeated by his NCOs in such a shower of commands that order was immediately restored.

The garrison leaves

At last it was time to leave. When everyone was ready, Lieutenant Roy ordered the first barricade in the western tunnel to be dismantled and German pioneers took down the second barricade. Knowing the fort to be dark, Captain Gillhausen had ordered them to take lanterns with them and seeing the line of lights stretching down the tunnel, Müller was reminded of honour guards at ceremonial events in Germany before the war. A German rifleman was told off to count the men aloud as they passed and, one by one, with officers in the lead, the men of Fort Vaux began to make their way out. The final count was eleven officers and 447 men unwounded, twenty-nine medical personnel and eighty-seven wounded. With the fit men helping the wounded along, they shuffled slowly through the narrow tunnel, struggling through the German pioneers, gunners and infantry who were already moving up into the barracks. Pausing at the observation post, they gathered their last strength for the long descent to the ditch and the slow, painful climb up to the ditch bunker. As the first man entered the bunker there

Members of the German 53rd Infantry Regiment in a barrack room in Fort Vaux. *Marcus Massing*

was a sharp command of *Achtung!* and a squad of German soldiers presented arms, watching wide-eyed as the long line of filthy and ragged men staggered past them into the open air.

To men who had been shut inside for days, the sudden daylight was blinding. Larks were singing but the joyful cascade of notes went unnoticed. All they wanted was water. The Germans had promised them water when they reached the bottom of the hill but that was too far for men who were mad with thirst and many simply tottered to the nearest shell hole and drank madly. Fearing that the prisoners were trying to escape, the Germans fired shots in the air and the exasperated escort was strengthened. Staggering and stumbling, the garrison was moved along. None of them had

Joseph Coste, the bugler of Fort Vaux, is remembered in the central square of his home town, Villelongue de la Salanque, in southwest France. *Author's collection*

Zouaves in the uniform of 1914. By 1916 they had adopted a khaki coloured version of standard French infantry uniform, plus steel helmet.
Tom Gudmestad

seen this side of Vaux Hill before and they stared in disbelief and horror at what they now saw. Three months of constant shelling had turned the hillside into unimaginable confusion. Shell craters, trenches, dugouts, wire, tools, personal equipment, scraps of uniform and corpses, some several months old, littered the ground as far as the eye could see. But it was not only the French who stared; news of the surrender had spread like wildfire and everyone who could do so came out to watch them pass. Finally arriving at the bottom of the hill they entered a ruined farmyard where the Germans had prepared great tubs of water. It was faintly flavoured with coffee and at last there was enough for every man to drink as much as he could, and then drink and drink again.

Major Raynal leaves Fort Vaux

Not everyone left the fort when the garrison did. Raynal and Alirol remained behind to arrange for the transport of the wounded and the burial of the dead. Then, when everything was finished, they too began the long journey down Vaux Hill. They were accompanied by QuiQui, the little black and white dog, who had also survived the siege. As they were leaving, a rifleman shouted to Raynal in thick German dialect that he should take his coat off: Vaux Hill was tough going and the journey would make him sweat. Amused, Raynal accepted the advice and it was in the khaki-coloured uniform of an officer of a colonial regiment that the former commandant of Fort Vaux made his way into German captivity. Later, he was taken to the headquarters of General von Engelbrechten, the commander of 50th Division, who expressed admiration for Raynal's defence of the fort and assured him that no shame attached to the defeat. Hardly able to believe his ears, Raynal proudly retorted that the Germans had nothing to do with it: thirst alone had defeated the garrison. The following day he was again taken to meet a senior commander, this time Crown Prince William of Germany. The Crown Prince, who spoke fluent French, also congratulated him on the fort's brave defence and, as Raynal had no sword, offered him the sword of another French officer. Not wishing to explain that he had arrived at Fort Vaux with only a walking stick, Raynal accepted the sword and left for prison camp in Maintz, taking QuiQui with him.

The Germans were jubilant. After more than three months of superhuman effort they were finally in control of the vital defensive work. Inspecting Fort Vaux, they found to their joy that they had not only acquired a substantial number of guns, but also huge stores of ammunition, explosives, medical supplies and food. With a French attack expected at any moment, infantry and pioneers spread out around the fort. Machine guns were set up in the Bourges Casemates,

Major Raynal, centre, with Lieutenant Alirol, right, and an unknown German officer. *Collection Vieillot*

ditch bunkers and barrack rooms and throughout the day the new defenders waited for the assault.

The final relief attempt

It came at 4.30am next morning. The French had no way of knowing what had happened in Fort Vaux on 7 June until informed of it by a German communiqué. Even then, they did not believe it; General Nivelle had already issued orders for another relief attempt to be made on 8 June and he saw no reason to change his mind. The new operation was to be led by Colonel Savy, commander of the elite 4th Moroccan Brigade, and composed of units from the 2nd Zouaves and Moroccan Colonial Infantry (MCI), who at the time were holding the second line on the Left Bank. Ignoring protests from staff officers that an attack carried out by tired troops who did not know one another and had been hastily brought together under an unknown commander on unfamiliar, shattered and debris-strewn ground would be unlikely to succeed, Nivelle pressed ahead. In the early hours of 7 June, reconnaissance officers inspected their positions and later that day the troops were brought by lorry to the Right Bank. Drawing ammunition and rations, they set off for the front but an enemy bombardment and the appalling difficulty of the heavily shelled ground meant that, when zero hour arrived, few of the units were in place. In addition, the Germans attacked before everyone was ready and, although they were driven off, the unexpected action put an increased strain on the already exhausted troops. Despite that, the order to attack was maintained. Moving forward, the Zouaves were caught in a monstrous barrage and with the battalion commander and all his officers killed, a second lieutenant took command and ordered the survivors back. At the same time some of the MCI managed to reach the south ditch, where they were pinned down by machine gun fire and unable to advance. With 90 per cent of their officers out of action and companies reduced to twenty-five men, they too returned to their starting point.

It was over. For the moment there would be no more attempts to retake Fort Vaux. Putting a brave face on the loss, the French radio station in the Eiffel Tower broadcast the following message during the evening of 8 June: *After seven days of long and bitter struggle against attacking forces relieved at will, the garrison of Fort Vaux, at the end of its strength, could no longer prevent the Germans from occupying the fort, which devastating artillery fire had completely destroyed. French troops hold the immediate approaches to the fort and the trenches to left and right and are repelling all German assaults.*

But nothing could disguise the fact that a second fort in the main line of resistance at Verdun had fallen to the Germans, thus providing them with another safe haven immediately in the rear of their front lines.

The loss of Fort Vaux was a devastating blow to the French and it was not just a blow to morale. With the threat to their right flank removed, the Germans could be expected to do all they could to break the French resistance at Verdun once and for all. With General Joffre retaining as many resources as he could for the coming Allied offensive on the Somme, there would be no reinforcements to meet the expected operations: the Army of Verdun was on its own. At the beginning of June General Pétain, who had been moved to command the Group of Armies of the Centre while retaining general control of events at Verdun, had made it clear that the high ground on the Right Bank must be held at all costs in order to prevent the Germans from threatening the Meuse bridges. This was followed on 4 June by a note from General Nivelle, informing his commanders that 'we should not take so much as one step back ... even if that means we must die where we stand'. In fact, despite his firm stance, General Nivelle had already begun to consider the possibility of evacuation to the unfinished Fourth Line on the Left Bank and had asked his officers to report on the feasibility of such a move, while insisting that there should be no movement without his express order. However, on 8 June there came news of a worrying withdrawal from the French line. On that day, boosted by the capture of a second French fort, the Germans had launched another attempt to push the lines away from Fort Douaumont. Swamped by the onrushing flood of Germans and with only a handful of men left to hold the chaotic positions, two young lieutenants of the 347th Infantry, Herduin and Millant, ignored General Nivelle's clear orders and pulled their remaining men out of the line. Contact with the units on either side was lost and

The memorial to Lieutenants Herduin and Millant inaugurated in November 2009. It stands close to the chapel of Fleury-devant-Douaumont.
Author's collection

with the French defence of the Right Bank hanging by a thread, the two young officers were shot without trial. In a note issued on 10 June, General Nivelle informed his commanders that the act of retreating 'would be a crime'. No more ground was given up. (Lieutenant Pierre Millant is buried in front of the Ossuary in plot 6177.)

Lessons learnt from the fall of Fort Vaux

With other forts and fieldworks likely to come under German attack in the near future, General Nivelle quickly issued a list of the lessons to

The central memorial in the German cemetery at Bouligny, northeast of Verdun, which contains many 50th Division graves. *Author's collection*

be learned from the fall of the fort. In a note dated 12 June he ascribed the fall to various factors: disarmament of the Bourges Casemates; abandonment of Ditch Bunkers 1 and 2; the absence of machine guns on the superstructure; and the lack of water. However, his main recommendations concerned the garrison. In future, only the official garrison of a fort or fieldwork was to be allowed to remain inside and any ammunition stored there was for garrison use only. When it was clear that an assault was imminent, commandants should ensure that they had sufficient supplies of food, water and ammunition. Internal corridors and tunnels that could not be covered by machine guns should be blocked off. A protected signalling station should be set up and steps taken to defend the garrison from attacks by gas and flamethrowers. In addition, all superfluous troops should be expelled and under no circumstances should external troops be supplied with water. If threatened with encirclement, commandants were to use *every available means* – the use of italics in the document indicating the seriousness of the threat – to prevent battlefield refugees from entering, as their arrival was a demoralizing factor and they would consume the available supplies. Nivelle also recommended the establishment of direct liaison between fixed fortifications and the appropriate gun batteries, with agreed signals that could bring down light calibre fire on the superstructure as soon as the garrison had taken shelter inside.

In the end, however, as General Nivelle recognized, the best guarantee of resistance was the personality of the commandant and he ascribed any moments of despair in Fort Vaux to the superfluous men rather than to the garrison, whose morale had remained high at all times. This he **General Nivelle.** ascribed to Raynal's handling of the situation and his attitude which – again using italics – General Nivelle referred to as *sublime*.

German General Headquarters announces the surrender

Rather less than sublime was the German announcement about the fall of Fort Vaux. Remembering the embarrassment caused by the premature announcement of the fort's capture in March 1916, and the unrest that followed the award of decorations after the capture of Fort Douaumont on 25 February, staff at German General Headquarters waited until 7 June before officially reporting that Fort Vaux was in German hands. Unfortunately, the information on which the report was based was provided by an officer of the 158th Infantry and as a result it attributed the capture to that regiment alone, assisted by pioneers. To make matters worse, the announcement referred to Lieutenant Rackow as the overall leader of the assault and announced that Kaiser William had been pleased to award him the *Pour le Mérite*.

To the men of the 53rd Infantry, who had been the first to reach Fort Vaux in the early hours of 2 June, and to those of the 39th Fusiliers and 126th Infantry who had withstood the continuous bombardment and fought off repeated French assaults between 4 June and 7 June, this was a serious insult. Such were the protestations that on 9 June the divisional commander, General von Engelbrechten, issued an Order of the Day which acknowledged the part played by the 53rd and the Fusiliers and gave the latter regiment credit for bringing about the surrender. This offended the 126th Infantry even more and to soothe their ruffled feelings another Order of the Day was issued on 14 June, which finally acknowledged that the surrender of Fort Vaux had been brought about by the unshakeable courage of both the 39th Fusiliers and the 126th Infantry. However, no change was ever made to the first official announcement and for years the failure to make amends left bitter feelings with many men.

The pumping station near Tavannes Tunnel from where water was pumped to Fort Vaux until March 1916. *Author's collection*

Chapter Seven

FORT VAUX RETURNS TO FRENCH HANDS

The Germans organize the fort

While the French were coming to terms with the loss of Fort Vaux, the Germans were starting to organize it for long-term occupation. The 39th Fusiliers, whose losses between 4 June and 7 June had amounted to over 50 per cent, were withdrawn and replaced by the 143rd Infantry and within a few days a senior staff officer from 50th Division could report that matters were well in hand. The strength of Fort Vaux and the observation and signalling possibilities provided by its position at the eastern edge of the battlefield were supremely important to the Germans. From the Bourges Casemates and observation posts, infantry and artillery observers could look far out over the surrounding French positions and send back vital information to the units concerned. To emphasize its importance, an engineer officer was attached to the fort, answering directly to the commandant and responsible for organizing

The entrance to the unfinished German tunnel that was intended to provide access from Vaux Hill to the ditch close to Ditch Bunker No. 1. The dark oval shape at centre left is the tunnel mouth. On the right are the steps to Ditch Bunker No. 1; in the left foreground are rotting pit props.
Author's collection

Twenty three year old Corporal Louis Boutard, 132nd Infantry Regiment, is commemorated in this handsome memorial which stands scarcely 300 metres from the fort. He was killed on 21 June 1916, a victim of the German thrust away from Fort Vaux. *Author's collection*

repairs and directing building work – an early task was to investigate the rotating turret, which was cleared and turned into a signalling station. As the weeks went by, order was established. Depots were created for ammunition, hand grenades and pioneer supplies; there was a food store, a wireless station and a pigeon loft. With access to the fort subject to constant shelling and always extremely dangerous, work began on providing safe access by means of an underground tunnel that would run from Vaux Hill to the ditch close to Bunker No. 1 (see Tour No. 2). The first aid post was cleaned out and a doctor given responsibility for improving and maintaining conditions there. Under his direction an attempt was made to clean the latrines and, when that was not successful, to chlorinate them so heavily that they were not a danger to health.

With so many men inside the barracks and every opening sandbagged, the temperature inside soon rose to uncomfortable levels. The walls streamed with humidity, breathing was difficult and headaches frequent. Shelling brought sand, stones and cement down from the roof, drying men's eyes and parching their throats so much that no one could eat their rations of peppery tinned meat and sausage. Candles and paraffin lamps added smoke and carbon monoxide to the already thick air. The daily passage of so many men through the fort made it impossible to keep clean and rubbish of all sorts piled up in corridors and barrack rooms, combining with the presence of hundreds of unwashed and lice-ridden men, wounded and corpses, to produce a powerful stench. Most men would have found the conditions there intolerable had the barracks not offered some respite from the even worse conditions outside. As it was, throughout the summer of 1916 Fort Vaux provided rest, shelter and basic medical facilities to thousands of men, as well as safe accommodation for vital front line command and observation units.

With Fort Vaux strongly organized, the Germans could continue their thrust along the ridges towards Verdun. In a series of extremely costly offensives launched between 8 June and 11 July 1916 the Germans managed to push the front forward but in desperate fighting the French hung on and prevented a breakthrough to the next strategic point, the heights around Fort Souville. During the early summer General von Falkenhayn was forced to transfer resources away from Verdun to meet Allied offensives on the Eastern Front, in Italy and on the Somme. By mid-July, with losses mounting and resources ever more limited, Crown Prince William ordered his troops to go on the defensive. However, the French went on attacking and on 28 August 1916, impatient with the lack of success, the Kaiser asked for General von Falkenhayn's resignation and replaced him with Field Marshal von Hindenburg. Visiting Verdun within a few days of taking over, Hindenburg declared the battle to be a running sore and promptly ordered all operations to cease.

The French counter-offensive

By then the French were planning a major operation on the Right Bank that would recapture not only the lost forts but also the high ground held before the battle began. The man in charge of the operation was Charles Mangin, a career general well known for his aggressive qualities, and even before his plan was accepted the first steps had been taken. Preparing the battlefield was a gigantic task. The summer's desperate fighting had ground the battlefield to powder, which the autumn rains turned to sticky mud. Nevertheless, the work was pushed on as fast as possible. Facilities at railway stations in the rear were extended to receive the enormous quantities of ammunition and supplies that would be needed, while at the front troops laboured to

The La Lauffée fieldwork. Although situated less than two kilometres southeast of Fort Vaux, it remained in French hands throughout the Battle of Verdun. *Author's collection*

build or repair the starting positions. At the same time French guns kept up a steady bombardment on the German lines, preventing the troops from repairing their defences or erecting wire. With worn guns and limited artillery provision, the Germans were powerless to counter the steady French bombardment, which blew trenches and gun positions into the air as soon as they were built.

Despite the best efforts of infantry and pioneers, the German lines in the Vaux sector were merely a string of unconnected trenches supported by a few machine gun posts based on former French positions hurriedly redeveloped for German use. In the hope of encouraging the men to greater efforts, German commanders took the

Field Marshal von Hindenburg. *Author's collection*

120

extraordinary step of ordering that companies should not be relieved until they had completed their allotted tasks. Even that draconian measure could not improve matters. The problem was that 50th Division was simply exhausted. Its men had been fighting in the Vaux sector since April and had suffered almost 20,000 casualties but when, at the end of August, General von Deimling requested their withdrawal, it was refused. By then the men were at the end of their physical and nervous strength and the refusal made them dispirited and sullen. Morale was also affected by the constant transfer of units to other fronts and – as it was extremely rare for a company or platoon leader to have been with the regiment since the start of the battle – by the lack of experienced leaders. Matters were not improved by the fact that since mid-summer the number of available replacements had not only been insufficient to cover the losses suffered but had also included a substantial number of men with convictions for military offences, which posed a threat to discipline and *esprit de corps*. Unnerved German officers reported insubordination and mutinous behaviour when troops returned from the front and it took all the efforts of officers and military police – together with improvements to their wellbeing – to remind the men of their duty and the need for perseverance.

In the circumstances it was impossible to develop the planned secondary positions, so all efforts were concentrated on a few principal strongpoints, the most important of which was Fort Vaux. Despite being under fire for months, the barracks and observation posts remained usable and the fort was protected on all sides by machine guns. However, that could not compensate for the overall French superiority in men and material which – although the Germans did not know it yet – included two mighty 400mm railway howitzers, whose longer range and greater penetrating power made them more powerful than anything available to the Germans. Nicknamed 'Alsace' and 'Lorraine', the two guns had been brought up to specially constructed spur lines some fourteen kilometres southwest of Fort Vaux, where they waited under camouflage until needed.

They did not have to wait long. On 20 October an avalanche of fire blasted German front and rear positions, shattering communications and blowing men, trenches and guns into the air. Desperately the German front line infantry called for artillery support but in the Vaux sector, where ammunition was so scarce that batteries could only fire on brigade orders, none was forthcoming. Fort Vaux rocked and groaned under the onslaught as shell after shell roared down, blocking the main exit, caving in the underground tunnels and filling the barracks with dust and fumes that choked the garrison and put out the lights. Realizing that a major assault was imminent, all troops not needed to defend the fort were ordered out, while pioneers, infantry and machine gunners rushed to clear away the debris and barricade the underground tunnels.

General Charles Mangin. *Tony Noyes*

At 11.30am on 24 October the French jumped off. On the left of the front and in the centre the operation went well and by the end of the day Fort Douaumont was in French hands once more. However, on the right, where the 74th Division under General de Lardemelle was charged with retaking Fort Vaux, fierce German resistance held up the French advance and Fort Vaux remained in German hands. A furious General Mangin insisted that another attempt should be made the following day but once again it was unsuccessful and the French withdrew, leaving horizon-blue casualties covering the ground in all directions.

Inside Fort Vaux the garrison was jubilant. Compared to the French, their losses were small and their satisfaction was increased by a congratulatory message from Crown Prince William, praising them for their valiant defence of the position. However, the failure of the French assault did not mean that their troubles were over. Although the 74th Division had failed to recapture Fort Vaux on 24 October, they had retaken important high ground from which they could harass German troops in the sector and they now began a series of local operations aimed at gradually pushing the Germans back towards

Infantry Shelter LLM1, also known as PC Maroc. This strong shelter served as the divisional command post for 74th Division during the French counter-offensive of 24 October 1916 and subsequent days.
Author's collection

the edge of the hills. At the same time French guns raised their fire to hurricane levels. Despite that, morale in Fort Vaux remained high. The garrison was cut off but that did not prevent them from observing enemy movements and flashing messages to the rear. The fort commandant, Lieutenant Bellman, 192nd Infantry, was everywhere, talking to his men, encouraging them to greater efforts and ensuring the distribution of necessary supplies of ammunition, food and water. But the shelling went on and as, despite their ferocious resistance, the Germans were slowly pushed back, their commanders had to face giving up the positions so bloodily won. To do so was almost unthinkable. For almost five months the defence of Fort Vaux had demanded from all ranks the highest levels of courage and determination and to give it up now, after so much blood had been shed, was a dreadful blow. But, faced with their own depleted strength and overwhelming French superiority in men and material, there was no alternative. With heavy heart the German High Command decided that Fort Vaux and the positions on Vaux Hill should be evacuated. As far as possible Fort Vaux itself should be destroyed.

1 November

Even before the garrison knew about it, specialized pioneers carrying the necessary explosives and equipment were already on the way. Lorries dropped them some distance from Vaux Hill and it was with

The effect of heavy shelling on the barracks. This picture of Fort Vaux was taken while it was still in German hands. *H.P. von Müller's Estate*

the ground rocking and shaking under them that the pioneers picked their way through the darkness to the looming mass of the fort, the last German supply column to ascend Vaux Hill. At 6am on 1 November Captain Rosencrantz, 100th Pioneer Company, handed his orders to Lieutenant Bellman and work began. Charges were placed in the rotating turret, the observation posts, the powder magazines and all the tunnels, including the unfinished access tunnel to Vaux Hill. Shelling caused a number of casualties and hampered preparations but the work went on steadily until, in the early hours of 2 November, everything was in place.

By then the last German garrison had left Fort Vaux. They had received the evacuation order with a mixture of surprise and regret. For sixteen days the garrison had held out against repeated assaults and now, after so much effort, the fort was to be abandoned. Having destroyed the signal rockets and put the revolver guns out of action, they shared out as much of the remaining food and water as they could carry and tried to destroy what was left. Then, at 12.30am on 2 November, the men of the last German garrison made their way through the tunnel to Ditch Bunker No. 2, following the route taken by Major Raynal and his men so many months before. By 1am the only men left in Fort Vaux were the commandant and the pioneers. Thirty minutes later the explosions began. The commandant ignited the charge in the western observation post before Captain Rosencrantz blew the rotating turret into the air. For the next half hour Fort Vaux rang with massive explosions and the ground shook as stones and concrete rained down. By 2am it was all over and the pioneers packed up their equipment and left. When the last German commandant emerged from the ditch bunker and set off down Vaux Hill, the observation posts were demolished, the rotating turret lay in the ditch and thick black smoke was belching through gaping holes in the roof. Fort Vaux, for which so much blood had been spilt on both sides, lay empty, a smoking ruin open to the sky.

At 5pm on 2 November a German radio broadcast announced that Fort Vaux had been evacuated and immediately a French patrol, consisting of infantry accompanied by sappers carrying electric torches, tools and explosives, was ordered forward to investigate. Setting off with volunteers in the lead, they arrived at Fort Vaux at 1am and found that the enemy was nowhere to be seen. After some hesitation the first men scrambled across the ditch to look for a way in. No entrances were found on the superstructure but after some time an officer discovered an opening in the south ditch that had been blocked by sandbags. These were quickly pulled away and a lieutenant crawled inside. He was met by clouds of acrid smoke and signs of a hurried exit

Blown out on 2 November 1916, the cupola of the 75mm turret lies on the rampart above the north ditch. *H.P. von Müller's Estate*

but the enemy had gone. At 2.30am on 3 November 1916, after almost five months of German occupation, Fort Vaux was in French hands once more.

Some hours later the radio station in the Eiffel Tower broadcast the following message:

Yesterday, following several days of violent bombardment and without waiting for our infantry to attack, the enemy evacuated Fort Vaux, which had been coming under steadily increasing pressure. During the afternoon several loud explosions were heard in the fort and during the night our infantry, which was nearby, occupied this important work without loss. The external fortress ring at Verdun is now completely re-established and firmly held by our troops.

The Germans, of course, announced that both Fort Douaumont and Fort Vaux had been abandoned for more favourable positions prepared a long time in advance and less exposed to French artillery fire.

Over the next two days French troops pushed forward until they had re-established the positions originally held at the beginning of March 1916. They were a frightful sight. From Fort Vaux to the plain the ground was a vast sea of overlapping shell craters, smashed shelters and filthy, rotting debris. It was a vision of hell but it was French once more and with Fort Vaux safely in their hands again French commanders could begin to take stock and consider whether the Verdun forts had served their purpose.

After the Battle

The French soldiers who entered Fort Vaux on 3 November 1916 – like the military engineers who followed them – were surprised to find that although the fort was damaged, it was far from destroyed. The windows and doors on the south side of the barracks had been completely smashed, leaving gaping holes that had to be blocked up with massive sandbag barricades, but the thick concrete carapace on the roof had protected the building from months of bombardment by a type of heavy shell unimaginable when the fort was built. The underground tunnels, which were roofed with lighter, steel–reinforced concrete, had not survived so well but they had all had been repaired by the Germans, and despite the attempt to destroy the fort from inside, the Bourges Casemates and ditch bunkers were in reasonable condition and could be rearmed.

In December 1916 responsibility for repairing and rearming Fort Vaux passed to the Forts Department (*Service des Forts*), a specialized

The cupola today, still lying where it fell in 1916. *Author's collection*

A piece of the damaged rim of the 75mm turret, showing the great thickness of steel used. *Author's collection*

A view of the destroyed facade of the barracks after the fort's recapture by the French. *Tony Noyes*

unit set up by General Pétain to deal with technical questions concerning forts and fieldworks. Their first task was to clean up the damage caused by the internal explosions, strengthen the existing tunnels and investigate the stores of food, water and equipment – which included a generator – left behind by the Germans. Over the next few months engineers improved the water supply and sanitation, rearmed the ditch bunkers and turned the former rotating turret into a machine gun post. The wire entanglements on the glacis, which had been destroyed during the months of shellfire, were replaced by two new

128

fields of wire, each one ten metres deep. To ensure secure communication at all times in any future siege, a new series of deep tunnels was excavated to link the fort's vital organs – the Bourges Casemates, ditch bunkers and central command post – and to create a new remote access (see Tour No. 2). In the immediate surroundings of the fort the shattered ground was consolidated by dumping spoil from the tunnelling work, before a new communication trench and a mule/wagon path were created. Later a 40cm railway line was laid to bring supplies up to the entrance, electric lighting was installed and fans ensured the circulation of air. Thus repaired and strengthened, Fort Vaux continued to play an active part in the defence of Verdun up to the Armistice in November 1918.

Effect on French thinking

During the 1920s Fort Vaux was left in its wartime state and it quickly became a place of pilgrimage and tourism. It also became the centre of attention of military engineers from France and elsewhere, who were impressed by the resistance demonstrated by the concrete used in its construction. After the war it was estimated that Fort Vaux had been battered by 60,000 shells, many of which were of the heaviest calibre known at the time. None, however, had pierced the concrete carapace and this led to extensive studies of the effects of shellfire on different

A postwar view of the south side of the barracks, with the western Bourges Casemate in the upper left. The postcard caption incorrectly describes this as the north ditch. *Tom Gudmestad*

types of concrete. The Battle of Verdun had shown that a defensive work that presented a smooth, low profile and was buried under a thick layer of specially designed concrete resisted shelling well. However, experience had also shown that, however strong the roof might be, no fort could survive without adequate supplies of food and water, secure communication systems, safe underground access, ventilation and defence against gas. These findings had a profound influence on French military thinking in the postwar years and, together with the memory of the 1,350,000 Frenchmen killed by enemy action during the First World War, they resulted in the decision to protect France from future German invasions by building another chain of ultra-modern, sunken forts along its eastern border. This was the Maginot Line, named after André Maginot, a Verdun veteran seriously wounded in November 1914, who, as Minister of Defence in 1930, was responsible for the adoption of the law proposing its creation. The new line was successful in dissuading the Germans from attacking France from the east and in 1940 they struck at France through Belgium, which gave the great sunken forts no opportunity to prove their strength.

With the construction of the Maginot Line, Fort Vaux ceased to be a vital front line stronghold. However, it retained a military role and, faced with the rising power of Germany during the 1930s, the French took steps to strengthen certain of its defensive elements, including the Bourges Casemates and the underground tunnels. Despite that, on 15 June 1940 Fort Vaux fell again to the Germans after a few hours' resistance. During the Second World War it remained open for German tourists and was visited by many soldiers who were curious to see the site of the famous siege. Fort Vaux was listed as a historic monument in 1970 and it remains the property of the French State.

June 1940: Fort Vaux is once again in German hands and the French garrison prepares to leave. *Marcus Massing*

EPILOGUE

Sylvain-Eugène Raynal did not live to see the outbreak of the Second World War. On 13 January 1939 he died of a heart attack at Boulogne-Billancourt, a suburb of Paris, and was buried three days later in the nearby cemetery of Bagneux. A detachment of soldiers presented arms as the hearse passed and his coffin was escorted by officers who had served at Verdun. A soldier through and through, Raynal returned to the army within weeks of the Armistice and saw several more years of service in France and Syria, being promoted to the rank of colonel in 1925. In 1926 he was again cited in Army Orders, this time for action in the Jebel Druze. He finally retired in 1931 and took part in the peace pilgrimage of April 1936, which brought him back to Fort Vaux. Of his former companions in adversity, Léon Buffet saw the fiftieth anniversary of the battle, dying in October 1966 just ten days short of his 70th birthday. Buffet became a teacher after the war and over the years many of his former pupils have been inspired to visit Fort Vaux and to reflect on the courage of the man they knew as an extraordinary professor of mathematics. His companion on the return journey,

Sergeant Fretté, who was seriously wounded, also survived but like many veterans he never spoke of his experiences. Joseph Coste, the bugler, returned to his native village of Villelongue de la Salanque in southwestern France, where the central square is named after him. There, a commemorative plaque describes Coste as standing on top of the fort 'amid shot and shell, blowing fit to burst his lungs' and no doubt that was how he remembered the event.

So many others did not live to see peace return. After the war a grieving French mother placed a touching memorial to her son on the facade of Fort Vaux. It read: *To my son, since your eyes closed, mine have never ceased to weep.* In an attempt to steal the memorial, thieves broke the plaque and today only a small piece remains. There is nothing to draw the eye to what is left and the broken plaque has never been replaced. The memorial to Captain Tabourot has also disappeared. Over the years visitor numbers have declined and at the time of writing the tourist bus from Verdun does not stop at Fort Vaux. Today's visitor will find a barracks that is empty, silent and damp. Time has passed, and with it has faded the memory of the heroism, suffering and sheer human effort of the extraordinary men on both sides who, in that fateful week of June 1916, fought the fight of moles and fought it well.

All that is left of the memorial plaque to a lost son on the façade of Fort Vaux. *Author's collection*

132

TOUR NO. 1

FORT VAUX OUTSIDE

Duration: One hour

The road that leads to Fort Vaux follows the approach taken by the French counter-offensive of October 1916. For months the area had been ploughed by shells of every calibre, including the giant 400mm and 420mm projectiles hurled by both sides. Under their terrible pounding, woods, buildings and roads vanished, while soil and stones were blasted into powder, which the autumn rains turned to deep, sticky mud. The result was a vast and devastated wasteland, a lunar landscape of overlapping shell craters and slippery earth that changed shape with every bombardment. Under the constant rain of shells it became a landscape without reference points, in which men heavily loaded with packs, rifles, personal equipment and any supplies needed for the front slowly made their way forward, hoping to avoid the shells

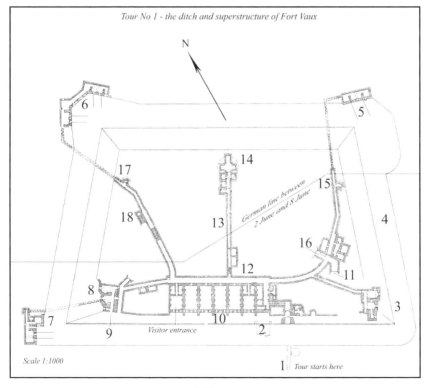

Tour No 1 - the ditch and superstructure of Fort Vaux

and desperately trying to stay on solid ground, because any man who slipped into the mud was lost. Not everyone was successful and as the weeks went by the Vaux sector became covered with every type of human and material debris until it resembled nothing so much as a vast rubbish dump that stretched for hundreds of metres in all directions.

Officially named Fort Dillon after an Irish regiment in the service of the kings of France before the Revolution, the defensive work you are about to visit has always been known as Fort Vaux.

Entrée de Guerre, or 'wartime entrance' – 1

The tour begins at the former *Entrée de Guerre*, or underground entrance to Fort Vaux, which is situated in the grassy dip between the main car park and the parking emplacements close to the barracks. Before 1916 wagons and supplies arriving here by road – the same route followed by vehicles today – arrived at the glacis on this side of the fort and passed through the wire. They then continued either to the main 'peacetime' entrance or entered the barracks by this tunnel. Men and supplies entering here were checked at the guard room, which is in the tunnel on the right. A flight of steps led from here into the barracks, so wagons could not go further than the second gates. All the gates to

Inside the wartime entrance looking out. During the siege of Fort Vaux this entrance was barricaded. *Author's collection*

A view of the south side of the barracks showing the sandbags used to block up the destroyed doors and windows after the French recaptured the fort. *Author's collection*

be seen are original. During the siege this entrance was strongly barricaded. **The wartime entrance may be visited but a torch is needed and visitors should be aware that the floor is uneven and slippery.**

Now stand where you have a good view of the front of the barracks. Note the massive layer of protective concrete that was poured on to the building during the modernization process of 1888. The layers created by the continuous pour process can be seen above the archways.

This is the south side of the fort. The ditch that originally protected the barracks on this side was filled in during 1917–18, when the spoil from the French tunnelling work under the fort was dumped here. As originally designed, the wide archways, which with one exception allowed access to the barrack rooms inside, enclosed two long windows and a door. The loopholed wall that protected these openings ran parallel with the front of the barracks. The position and width of the 'balcony' of the fort is roughly shown by the area of paler paving to be seen between the barracks and the grey surface of the parking area. This protective wall was a unique feature in Verdun fortifications but it was not concreted and it was soon destroyed, as were many of the doors and windows in the archways. The resulting yawning gaps were blocked up with loopholed sandbag barricades and strong fire from here helped to prevent the Germans from gaining control of this side of the fort. When the French retook Fort Vaux, they blocked up the archways permanently and added the embrasures to be seen today. Note that the archway to the left of the 'pigeon' plaque was always blank and appears only to have been included in the 1888 façade for reasons of architectural harmony.

Entrée de Paix, or 'peacetime entrance' – 2

Before the First World War the main entrance to Fort Vaux – and the only wagon access – was reached by a drawbridge that crossed over the ditch and passed through a gate in the loopholed wall. The gate was situated roughly where the pigeon plaque now stands. The guard room was in the small domed room to the right of the plaque. There was no internal access between the guard room and the barracks. The brick chimney to which the plaque is attached was added between the wars, when conscripts acting as guides lived in the barracks. The fort also had a civilian guide who lived in a house that stood at the entrance to the current car park. The two plaques on the barracks and other features on this side of the fort will be described later in the tour.

Eastern Bourges Casemate – 3

From here, turn right and walk along the front of the barracks to the well-preserved concrete bunker that overlooks the eastern ditch. Face the gun embrasures. This is a Bourges Casemate, a type of gun position that was first adopted in 1899 as a means of covering the intervals between forts and fieldworks. It was built of steel-reinforced concrete.

A postwar view of the eastern Bourges Casemate, with temporary graves.
Author's collection

The lower floor offered space for storage and ammunition and from there a concrete passage ran into the barracks. The guns were housed in two separate rooms that were arranged in echelon and protected from direct fire by the long wall on the right, which formed a protective wing. Each room mounted one 75mm field gun that was attached to a guide rail and could be moved to right or left. With a vertical elevation of approximately 14.5 degrees (from –7°.30' to +7°.16'), a horizontal field of fire of 64 degrees and a range of 4000 metres, the two guns here covered an extensive area to the east and southeast of Fort Vaux until they were removed in 1915.

When General Pétain took command at Verdun, he ordered the Bourges Casemates to be rearmed but the constant bombardment made it impossible. Machine guns were installed here instead and during the siege they performed a vital service in preventing the Germans from surrounding the fort and linking up with troops on the other side. When the French retook the fort, they found the Bourges Casemates to be damaged but not destroyed and, following various internal repairs, they were rearmed with 75s and provided with a substantial store of ammunition. Rebuilt during the 1930s to provide back-up for the Maginot Line, this one looks much as it did before 1914, although the observation post, which stood to the left of the gun rooms, was not rebuilt. It is not open to the public.

The eastern ditch – 4

From here, go down into the ditch and walk towards the bunker ahead. Before the Battle of Verdun all the ditches surrounding Fort Vaux had high vertical walls that were revetted with dressed stone on both sides. The walls were completely smashed by shelling and no trace of the revetment remains today. There is also no trace of the picket posts and wire with which the French protected the ditch after November 1916.

The ditch at Fort Belleville, another of the Verdun forts, is also revetted with dressed stone on both sides. The ditch at Fort Vaux would have looked like this. *Author's collection*

During the battle men who died or were injured in these ditches stayed where they fell, as the constant shellfire made it too difficult to remove them.

Ditch Bunker No. 1 – 5

At the bunker, stop and face the front. The eastern observation post is now at the top of the rampart behind you. During the siege the German line on this side of the fort crossed the ditch roughly level with this observation post.

Before Fort Vaux was modernized in 1888 these ditches were defended by caponiers – small bastions built of stone which stood at the inner corners of the ditch and were loopholed for rifle fire. During the rebuilding phase the caponiers were demolished and replaced by three strong concrete bunkers, which were embedded in the outer corners of the ditch and roofed with a massive layer of reinforced concrete. The battered structure to be seen here originally comprised two rooms. From the room on the left – which provided accommodation for the defenders – a long flight of steps led to the tunnel into the barracks. The guns stood in the room on the right. It was through this bunker that Major Raynal entered Fort Vaux on 24 May 1916.

When the Germans attacked on 2 June 1916, the guns here – machine guns, revolver guns and light cannon – covered the eastern ditch. The doors were blocked up with sandbags. The Germans could not attack the bunker from the ditch as the covering fire from Bunker No. 2, visible some 200 metres to your left, was too violent to allow them to approach it from this side. Having got inside through the breach in the rear wall, they were delighted to find that, in addition to guns and ammunition, the bunker contained substantial stores of food, clothing and shoes. While some men read the graffiti and admired the drawings that covered the walls, others divided up the unexpected spoils, throwing anything they could not use into the ditch.

With Fort Vaux constantly under fire, entering and leaving was fraught with danger at all times and many men were lost before they got this far. In an attempt to provide secure access, the Germans began work on a tunnel starting at a complex of dugouts on Vaux Hill and ending under the ditch here. Four shafts were sunk during August 1916 but the tunnelling required such effort that by the end of October only 40 metres had been completed. The tunnel was destroyed by the French after November 1916. There is no external access to this bunker today, nor any trace of the makeshift breach in the rear wall defended by

A postwar postcard view of the destroyed 75mm turret, rebuilt as a machine gun post. *Author's collection*

The same view in 2010. *Author's collection*

Captain Tabourot and his men in the early hours of 2 June. The plaque to Captain Tabourot, to be seen on some old views of the bunker, has also disappeared.

From here, continue along the northern ditch towards Ditch Bunker No. 2. The German assault of 2 June 1916 came in on this side of the fort and the first men to reach the superstructure managed to cross this ditch before Bunker No. 2 began firing. As you walk along, the damaged 75mm turret will come into view on the rampart to your left, with the cupola and parts of the shattered turret rim lying on the slope. This turret is covered later in this tour. When you reach the bunker, stop and face the front.

Ditch Bunker No. 2 – 6

This bunker controlled the northern and western sides of the ditch and was connected to the barracks by a tunnel that entered the bunker at the left-hand end. It was armed in the same way as Ditch Bunker No. 1 and it was here that the storm pioneers lay on the top to poke their short flamethrowers into the gun ports. The bunker is inaccessible today but by peering under the bushes that grow against it visitors will glimpse the devastation wrought by the huge 420mm shells in February 1916. It will also give an idea of the state of the bunker during the siege, when it served as the German command post. It was to this bunker that a delighted Lieutenant Müller ran to find Captain Gillhausen with Raynal's letter of surrender. There is no trace today of the breach that allowed the Germans entry on 2 June 1916.

Ditch Bunker No. 3 – 7

From here, continue along the western ditch to Ditch Bunker No. 3, which is at the end on the right. During the siege the German line crossed this ditch roughly two-thirds of the way along. Pass the western Bourges Casemate (above you on the left) and face the bunker, the entrance to which is below normal ditch level. The increased depth provided extra protection from attackers and also a space into which debris could fall without blocking doors or embrasures. Before the

A postwar view of the western ditch looking towards Ditch Bunker No. 2. The western Bourges Casemate is at the top of the rampart to the right, just out of the picture. *Author's collection*

Battle of Verdun all the ditch bunkers here had extra ditches in front of the entrances but in the case of Ditch Bunkers 1 and 2, these 'drop ditches' have been filled up. Unlike the two bunkers you have just seen, this one remained in French hands throughout the siege and the guns here – which controlled the south side of the fort – not only prevented the Germans from occupying the ditch in front of the barracks but forced any men on the superstructure to keep their heads down. It comprised two rooms and was unusual in having an internal latrine. There is no external access but from the right-hand end a tunnel still runs under the ditch into the Bourges Casemate behind you.

Western Bourges Casemate – 8

Now go up the steps to the western Bourges Casemate and face the guns. This casemate was also rebuilt in the 1930s and looks very much

The western ditch today, with Ditch Bunker No. 3 in the left foreground and the western Bourges Casemate on the right. *Author's collection*

as it did before the Battle of Verdun, with two gun rooms in echelon and an observation post on the right. With a horizontal field of fire of 45 degrees, the guns here commanded the French positions between Hardaumont and Bazil Ravine, all of which were attacked repeatedly by the Germans between March and June 1916. The Hardaumont positions are on the far skyline to your left rear and the Germans were attacking downhill from there. By March 1916 the 75s originally mounted here had been replaced by machine guns and it was they that tore such holes in the German ranks on 1 June. When they retook the fort, the French left the machine guns in place but later armed this casemate with 75mm guns similar to those in position today. It is open to the public and will be visited in Tour No. 2.

The western end of the barracks, with the western Bourges Casemate. The peace envoys left the barracks through the second doorway on the left.
Author's collection

Buffet's escape – 9

Now follow the footpath round to the front of the barracks and stop at the first entrance, which is closed by a steel grille. Face the barracks, noting the difference in height between where you are now standing and the ditch to your left. It was through a small window in this area of the barracks that Buffet and a handful of others escaped on 4 June. Having climbed out, they had to cross the 'balcony', drop into the ditch and cross it before scrambling up the other side and making off across the glacis – all without attracting the attention of the Germans on the roof! In such circumstances, the chances of many men making it out safely were very small and the War Diary of Fort Tavannes only reports the arrival of about a dozen. Rebuilding in this part of the barracks means that it is impossible to identify the exact place of exit.

A short distance further on a second grille covers the exit through which Lieutenant Bénazet and the bugler left the barracks with Raynal's letter of surrender, returning shortly afterwards with Lieutenant Müller.

From here, continue along the front of the barracks. The two arched openings that you pass before reaching the visitor entrance originally housed the peacetime military telegraph and the garrison workshop, both of which only had external access. The walls that partially block the entrances were built after the French retook the fort. Pass the visitor entrance, to which you will return later. The huge chunks of steel to be seen there are pieces of the broken rim of the rotating turret that was blown up by the Germans on 2 November 1916. As you walk ahead, note the huge thickness of the concrete layer added to the barracks during the modernization process in 1888.

Defenders' plaque – 10

Continue to the defenders' plaque, which features a gold sword and a laurel wreath. It was donated by the Association of Defenders of Fort Vaux and the text below the sword reads as follows:

For seven days (from 1 June to 7 June 1916) 250 men held out in this ruined fort against furious German assaults, attacks by gas and burning liquids, and the tortures of thirst.

The garrison was composed of detachments from the following units:

6 and 7 Companies, 142nd Infantry

3 Machine Gun Company, 142nd Infantry

3 Machine Gun Company, 53rd Infantry

Sappers, 2nd and 9th Engineers

Gunners, 5th Foot Artillery and 6th Artillery

Medical staff, 101st Infantry.

Beneath this inscription is the official surrender document, which is translated in Chapter 5. Note that on the plaque the surrender document is dated 7 June 1916 although Raynal actually dated it 7 May 1916.

The defenders' plaque.
Author's collection

Pigeon plaque

From here, continue to the 'pigeon plaque'. The steel door set in the archway before the plaque provided visitor access to the barracks during the 1930s.

Raynal's last pigeon, known as Valiant, died soon after arriving at the Verdun Citadel. Some months later a stuffed pigeon, said to be the same bird, was awarded a leg ring in the colours of the Legion of Honour and put on display. The inscriptions read as follows:

TO THE PIGEON BREEDERS

WHO DIED FOR FRANCE

TO THE PIGEON OF VERDUN

During the Battle of Verdun Major Raynal's last homing pigeon (No. 787–15) left this fort on 4 June 1916, carrying the following message: *We are still holding on but attacked by deadly gas and smoke. Urgent relief is vital. Request immediate blinker communication with Souville, which is not*

A popular postcard view of Raynal's last pigeon, No 787-15. The message is in Raynal's own handwriting. *Author's collection*

143

replying to our messages. This is my last pigeon. The pigeon accomplished its task and obtained the following citation:

> *Sole means of communication available to the heroic defender of Fort Vaux, it accomplished the task with which it had been entrusted by Major Raynal by transmitting the latest information to have been received by that officer, despite great difficulties caused by intense smoke and thick clouds of gas. Gravely intoxicated by gas, it arrived dying at the pigeon loft.*

> (*From the Diploma accompanying the award of the leg ring*)

This plaque was erected with donations from the pigeon-breeder associations of France, the Friends of Homing Pigeons and the 'Pigeon of Verdun' (Society of Verdun pigeon-breeders). It was inaugurated on 24 June 1929.

The exit from the eastern tunnel with the small blockhouse on the left and the eastern Bourges Casemate on the right. *Author's collection*

Small blockhouse

The small blockhouse attached to the barracks a few steps further on was built after the French recaptured the fort. It housed machine guns for the close defence of this side of the barracks. The small remnant of the broken memorial plaque mentioned in the Epilogue is to be found on the side facing the car park.

Exit from the eastern tunnel – 11

A short distance further on a footpath with steps leads to the top of the fort. Stop at the foot of the path and look ahead. The blockhouse in front of you marks the entrance to the passage across the eastern tunnel, which allowed access from this side of the fort to the inner courtyard. Now look towards the rear of the Bourges Casemate. The primers to be used in blowing up the fort's vital organs at the start of the Battle of Verdun were stored in two small rooms that used to stand

here on the right. They were destroyed by shelling on 26 February 1916 and without them the firing officer could not carry out his orders. The two rooms were not rebuilt.

The superstructure – 12

Now follow the path to the flagpole on top of the barracks. From here you have a clear view of the damage to the fort and its surroundings caused by shellfire during the Battle of Verdun. First, face the approach road to the fort. To your left the views that stretch eastwards for miles over the plain leave no doubt about why this site was so important to the French for observation and defence. Fort Souville – a high, tree-covered mound visible from here in winter – is roughly three kilometres to your right front. Now stand with your back to the approach road. The Hardaumont fieldworks, from which the Germans launched their attack on 8 March 1916, are buried in the trees on the distant skyline ahead. Fort Douaumont and the Ossuary stand on the same skyline some three kilometres to your left front. Seen from here, the Ossuary tower stands out better than the flagpole on the top of Fort Douaumont, which is only visible in really clear weather. The low rectangular construction by the flagpole was built after the battle and would not have been shell-proof. The orientation table that used to stand on the adjacent circular base was stolen long ago.

One of the two mild steel observation domes that originally stood on the top of the barracks and provided observation towards the south. *Author's collection*

Inner courtyard – 13

Now follow the footpath to the former rotating gun turret, which is directly in front of you. Between the flagpole and the turret the path passes through the inner courtyard of the fort, which has been filled with debris from the battle. At the foot of the turret is a mild steel observation dome which rather resembles an enormous medieval helmet. Between 1904 and 1906 three heavy steel domes were installed on observation posts on the north side of

Looking up the shaft of an observation post at the Ouvrage de la Falouse.
Author's collection

145

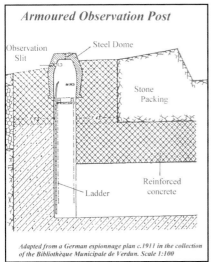

Armoured Observation Post

Observation Slit
Steel Dome
Stone Packing
Reinforced concrete
Ladder

Adapted from a German espionnage plan c.1911 in the collection of the Bibliothèque Municipale de Verdun. Scale 1:100

A similar light observation dome in position at the Ouvrage de la Falouse. *Author's collection*

the fort, covering the direction from which the enemy was most likely to come. In a further development before 1914, two lighter models – of which this is one – were also installed at each end of the barracks, facing south.

The former rotating gun turret and observation post – 14

Follow the footpath to the top of the turret and stop. The small steel dome set in concrete protects the observation post built by the French to replace the original post, which was destroyed in the German explosion of 2 November 1916. The dome, which is twenty-five centimetres thick and less than a metre wide, offered 240-degree vision through three slits that could be closed by shutters. It was reached by a ladder from inside and was very cramped. Inside, the observer perched on a small wooden seat while working with maps and binoculars to control and direct artillery fire. He communicated with the gunners by speaking tube. Experience during the Battle of Verdun showed that while these domes were strong in themselves, they could be blown out of the concrete by shells falling nearby. In addition, the slits did not close tightly enough to prevent observers from being concussed or even killed by the blast.

75mm Gun Turret

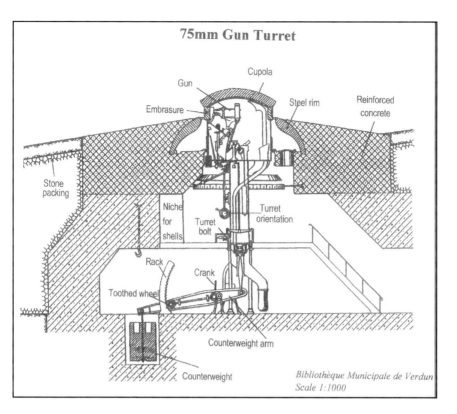

Gun
Cupola
Embrasure
Steel rim
Reinforced concrete
Stone packing
Niche for shells
Turret bolt
Turret orientation
Rack
Crank
Toothed wheel
Counterweight arm
Counterweight

Bibliothèque Municipale de Verdun
Scale 1:1000

The rotating steel gun turret installed here in 1904 was originally invented by Major Alfred Galopin in 1889. It mounted two 75mm guns with a maximum rate of fire of twenty-two rounds a minute and a range of 5,500 metres. The turret was activated by a vertical movement that raised it into the firing position and lowered it again once the guns had ceased firing. Raising the turret exposed the mouths of the gun barrels and allowed the guns to fire. When retracted, the gun barrels were hidden from view and entirely protected by a steel cupola some thirty centimetres thick, which proved strong enough to withstand even direct hits by the heaviest shells.

The turret was set in a wide pit in the top of a three-storey concrete unit that also housed magazines, replacement guns, range-finding equipment and the activating machinery. This comprised a steel beam some six metres in length which was attached at one end to a seven-ton counterweight and at the other end to a central column. The process of raising the turret began by turning two cranks on the steel beam, thus lowering the counterweight into a pit. The downward movement of the counterweight pushed the turret up into the firing position, where it was bolted into place. After firing, the bolts were withdrawn and the

The steel counterweight arm of an identical 75mm turret in Fort Marre, one of the Left Bank forts. *Author's collection*

cranks turned again, bringing the counterweight up and returning the turret to its original position. It took less than six seconds to raise the turret into the firing position. The guns were serviced by a team comprising an officer and up to eighteen men.

Following the accidental explosion of 26 February 1916, French army engineers wrote off this turret as irreparable. Major Raynal greatly regretted its loss, as the guns here would have allowed him to come to the aid of the French troops defending the hillsides below Hardaumont on 1 June 1916. When the Germans captured the fort they cleared the access tunnel and found that the guns were in good condition and that the turret could be raised, turned and lowered. Despite that, they only used it as a signalling station. The gun barrels were used to concentrate the beams of light from acetylene lamps that flashed messages to a receiving station to the northeast of the fort. Messages were normally sent in code but at times of great emergency encoding was dropped. It is easy to see that service under these turrets and observation domes during shelling was extremely stressful.

The eighty kilogram demolition charge placed here by the Germans on 2 November 1916 blew out the cupola, which lies between the turret and the ditch. All around lie segments of the massive steel rim that

The rebuilt 75mm turret. *Author's collection*

reinforced the edge of the turret pit. With the turret now completely beyond repair, the French covered the gaping hole with concrete and installed machine guns. It is inaccessible today but a similar turret may be seen at the newly restored *Ouvrage de la Falouse* (see Tour No. 4). Visitors wishing to see how an undamaged turret of this type looked from the outside should visit Fort Douaumont and the *Ouvrage de Froideterre*. Galopin turrets like this one were so advanced that they were used in the Maginot Line with only small modifications.

Eastern shoulder of the fort/eastern observation post – 15

Now walk towards the eastern observation post, whose emplacement is marked by a lone tree. The steel dome that originally protected this post was blown out during the bombardment of 26 February 1916 and further damage was caused by the explosions of 2 November. After recapturing the fort, the French covered the hole with a thick layer of concrete reinforced by steel joists and added a new observation slit.

Entrance to eastern tunnel – 16

From here look back along the footpath towards the barracks. The former entrance to the eastern tunnel from the inner courtyard is on the right below the footpath, roughly half-way between the barracks and

The eastern observation post rebuilt. *Author's collection*

where you are now standing. All that remains is a battered concrete wall, from which reinforcing bars protrude. It is generally covered by long grass in summer. It was there that the Germans attacked with flamethrowers on 5 June and it marks the limit of the German advance along the eastern tunnel. You will see the former entrance to your left as you return to the rotating turret.

Western shoulder of the fort/western observation post – 17

Now walk back towards the 75mm turret, go past it and continue to the western observation post, whose emplacement is covered by thorn bushes. Ditch Bunker No. 2 is in the corner of the ditch below. Although the steel dome that protected this post was not blown out in February 1916, the internal fittings were damaged by the blast from shells falling nearby and thereafter it could only be used with great care. It was from here on 1 June 1916 that Raynal observed the

149

Germans as they attacked downhill from Hardaumont and saw the devastating effect of the machine guns in the western Bourges Casemate. Blown out by the Germans in the first of the explosions of 2 November 1916, this post was later repaired by the French. It was in the tunnel below that Lieutenant Müller was told about the presence of French soldiers in the early hours of 7 June.

Exit from western tunnel – 18

From here, follow the footpath towards the western Bourges Casemate and stop by the bushes that grow on the left of the path about twenty metres ahead. These cover the entrance to the western tunnel from the inner courtyard. The repair work visible through the grille was carried out by the French after they retook the fort.

As this is the only external entrance to the western tunnel, it must have been there that Lieutenant Bénazet and the bugler brought their white flag to the Germans' attention. On the return journey, Bénazet and Müller crossed the top of the fort. As the passage into the barracks from the courtyard was blocked by a roof fall, the two men had to go round the western Bourges Casemate before diving into the barracks through the entrance noted earlier. The final German barricade in this tunnel was close to this entrance. That means that the distance between where you are now standing and Ditch Bunker No. 2 represents the entire German advance in the western tunnel between 2 June and 7 June 1916.

From here, return to the visitor entrance to begin Tour No. 2.

The facade of the barracks looking towards the small blockhouse and the eastern Bourges Casemate. The ditch has been filled up and the sandbagged openings replaced by concrete. *Author's collection*

The visitor entrance in 2010, looking like the entrance to a cave. The massive chunks of steel are from the destroyed 75mm turret. *Author's collection*

TOUR NO. 2

FORT VAUX INSIDE

Duration: one hour

NB: *The barracks are always cool and can be wet underfoot, so bring a sweater and wear stout footwear. A torch is also useful. While touring the barracks, see the plan on page xx.*

Visitor entrance and museum

The tour begins at the visitor entrance. Note the framed photographs of veterans of the siege and other memorabilia, particularly the aerial view of Fort Vaux in October 1916 and the photograph of General Pétain, rare at Verdun, on the end wall. Before the war this room was divided into three parts, with the larger part – towards the entrance – forming the kitchens. During the siege, when the rooms were used differently, it served as the ordnance store.

Continue into the fort's small museum, which is typical of the size and shape of the main barrack rooms and contains a selection of interesting artefacts. Note the brick ribbed arches that were added to strengthen the walls and roof during the modernization process in 1888. After the French retook the fort, the wall on the south side of the room was repaired with the embrasure to be seen today. The adjacent relief map shows the terrain on either side of the River Meuse and the

The fort's museum. *Author's collection*

position of the forts in the Verdun system. The hand-operated fan on the floor opposite the map is of the sort commonly used for ventilation in forts like this one. As you leave the museum, note the two gun barrels by the door. These are short-barrelled 75s of the type originally mounted in the rotating turret.

Water cisterns

From here, continue into the corridor and stop. In front of you a flight of steps leads down to the former water cisterns, which were originally reached by the steel ladder set in the deep wall niche. The steps were built after the French retook the fort and created the deep tunnel system, which can be accessed through the cisterns. The tunnel system is explained later in the tour.

The cisterns were designed to hold a total of 300 cubic metres (300,000 litres) of water, which was pumped to the fort from springs several kilometres away. During February and March 1916 shellfire cracked the cisterns and smashed the supply pipes, which could not be repaired during the battle. In May water fatigues brought up supplies in cans and barrels but the resulting reserve was uncertain – the figures referred to by Raynal and Lieutenant Roy differ by 15,000 litres. Water was also a preoccupation for the Germans and the stock of bottled water they brought up was tightly controlled. There was no water for washing or sanitation and any man who wanted more than his ration had to face the perils outside.

When the French recaptured the fort they solved the water problem by bringing up bottled mineral water. They also repaired one of the cisterns and used it, together with a number of metal tanks, to store approximately 30 cubic metres (30,000 litres) of drinking water.

However, this was only an emergency supply. Water needed for daily use was pumped to the fort from *Pré l'Evèque* (a large reservoir in Verdun close to the Citadel). French engineers also sank a well some forty metres below the fort, which provided more than 100 litres of water per hour. The concrete cistern suspended above the steps was built after the battle.

Main corridor and barrack rooms

Now turn right along the corridor, which is fifty metres long, two-and-a-half metres wide and roughly five metres high. Note the attachments for wooden benches along the lower left-hand wall. These are to be found in all the corridors and tunnels, right up to the ditch bunkers. The insulators attached to the keystones of many of the arches probably date from 1917–18.

The beds in the next two barrack rooms are similar to those used in 1916. When Lieutenant Roy arrived here with his sappers on 22 May he found three-tier beds in these rooms, which were dimly lit and crammed full of men. An incredible tangle of packs and belongings hung from the frames, while graffiti – names, dates, hearts and arrows, cheery messages for friends and insults for the enemy – covered every inch of woodwork. In 1913 Fort Vaux was connected to the electricity network, which provided lighting and ventilation, but by the time Roy arrived shellfire had smashed the supply cables and these rooms were lit by candles and paraffin lamps. In the third room traces of the original design are to be seen in the two blocked windows and central doorway in the end wall. Note also the section of 40cm railway line and remains of two small wagons to be seen along the foot of the wall. Lines and wagons such as these were used during the tunnelling operations under the fort, which are discussed later in this tour.

During the German occupation the first two rooms housed the sector reserves, who stood ready at all times to support the front lines. When the windows and doors at the end were blown out by shellfire, the gaping holes were blocked up with massive barricades of sandbags, which were fitted with embrasures for observation and defence. The barricades could be up to six metres in depth but shells regularly smashed through them, turning the barrack rooms into a bloodbath and filling the air with sand. If, as frequently happened on such occasions, a fire started, the doorway into the corridor was blocked up to prevent the smoke from spreading and to allow the fire to burn itself out. With sandbags also piled along the rear wall, there was little space left in these rooms and as a result most men camped in the corridor, which

was eventually fitted out with three-tier beds and benches.

To German troops arriving here on their way to the front the barracks resembled nothing so much as a giant ant heap, with men scurrying about in all directions. Here, they met units returning from the lines and for a short period the corridor rang with greetings, shouts and questions as men threw down their gear in the area assigned to them, looked for friends and comrades, swapped stories and passed on news. In such circumstances it required strong discipline to keep order and ensure that men who reached the safety of the fort did not simply remain behind in the maze of dark and overcrowded rooms and tunnels.

Once recaptured, the French cleared these rooms of dirt and debris and fitted them out for the new permanent garrison. Ammunition and food depots were established, while a generator provided electric light and powered fans to keep the air circulating.

A cross to remember the men who died in the fort before the surrender. The horizontal line on the wall to the left of the cross marks the original level of the floor. *Author's collection*

Above: Looking along the muddy access passage into the 75mm turret. *Author's collection*

Left: The stairway into the 75mm turret. *Author's collection*

Entrance to former rotating turret

Continue ahead to the entrance to the former rotating turret, which is on the left behind an iron grille. Note that the floor at the bottom of the steps has been dug up, perhaps to fill sandbags. The cross to be seen there is symbolic and represents all the men who died in the fort before it was surrendered. Beyond the cross the passage into the turret is obstructed by the steel reinforcing rods of the roof, which was smashed by a 420mm shell on 26 February 1916. The chunks of quicklime on the shelf to the right of the turret entrance were used to disinfect the latrines. At the time of writing an information panel in the western Bourges Casemate shows French troops engaged in repair work in the turret in November 1916.

Major Raynal's command post

Major Raynal's command post is a few steps further on. As originally designed, this barrack room was divided into three sections, with a large room at the back and a smaller one on either side of the central door, one of which was the communications room. According to Lieutenant Roy's annotated plan of the fort, which shows how the fort was used during the siege, the command post was not in the room with the window, as now shown, but in the larger area at the back. His account also refers to Raynal resting on a camp bed in his command post and there would be no space for that in the little room behind the window here. During the 1930s visitors entered the fort through the larger room at the back. Both French and German commandants used the same room as their command post.

First aid post

Turn right just beyond the command post. Before mobilization the first

A postwar view of the battered first aid post. *Author's collection*

155

room on the right was a food and clothing store but when war broke out it was fitted out as a first aid post with accommodation for six men lying and storage for medical supplies. During the siege this little post quickly became full and the doctors took over two of the neighbouring barrack rooms. Without water, wounds rapidly became infected and fever set in. It requires little effort to imagine the appalling conditions here, which the best efforts of the doctors could do little to alleviate. The medical staff included four doctors and three stretcher-bearers. Dr Conte and Dr Gaillard were both wounded in the siege.

Sand quarry

A short distance further ahead on the left a grating covers a hole broken through the original stone wall of the barracks. Visible beyond the hole is the layer of special concrete with which the fort was protected in 1888. The thick layer of sand that originally filled the gap between stone and concrete and acted as a shock absorber was used by the Germans for building and repair work during their occupation of the fort.

Commandant's sleeping quarters

This was originally the lamp store and Lieutenant Roy's plan does not show it to have been used as sleeping quarters during the siege. During the German occupation it was used by the fort's doctors.

Telephone exchange

This was originally the fuel depot. The fuel was brought up in barrels that fitted into slots still to be seen under the wooden bench.

The telephone system installed after the French recaptured the fort provided internal communication between the command post, barracks, observation posts and guns. The constant bombardment cut external telephone lines as soon as they were laid and as a result signalling lamps continued to be used for external communication.

Pigeon loft

The plan drawn by Lieutenant Roy puts the pigeon loft in approximately the same place as it is now, with a signalling station facing Fort Souville close by. Repair work in this area of Fort Vaux means that it is impossible to identify the site of the signalling station but it is clear from Raynal's account of the siege that it was close to his command post.

One of the two
entrances to the
150 metre long
tunnel that
provided safe
access to Fort Vaux
from a nearby
hillside.

Author's collection

The main gallery under the barracks,
with rooms off to the left.

Author's collection

In the tunnels under the barracks.

Author's collection

Tunnels, repairs and major excavation work

Go down the steps by the pigeon loft. When the first French soldiers crawled through the smoke and debris into Fort Vaux on 3 November 1916 they found – in addition to a sizeable store of food and bottled water – a Daimler engine, a 220 volt continuous-current dynamo and two Siemens drilling machines. The dynamo appeared to have been used for lighting the fort and all the machinery was in good condition. Over the next few days a complete report on the state of the fort internally and externally was drawn up and within a short time repair and rebuilding work began. The first task was to clean the barracks, cisterns and latrines of the mounds of dirt and debris that had accumulated during the battle. This was taken outside and dumped. Then the existing tunnels were cleared and repaired, with the tons of debris resulting from the internal explosions being used to consolidate the ground outside.

During the battle it quickly became clear that, while men were normally safe once they were inside a fort, entering or leaving it was fraught with danger. To deal with this problem, between 1917 and 1918 French military engineers created new, safer access routes into Fort Vaux in the form of two tunnels with exits at 150 metres and 800 metres away. In addition, a further series of deep tunnels linking the barracks to the rotating turret, ditch bunkers, Bourges Casemates and observation posts provided secure passage between the fort's vital organs at all times. As many men found life in the barracks during a bombardment to be extremely stressful, these tunnels included shelters as well as storage space. Tunnelling methods included modern mining equipment and blasting. The debris was evacuated in small wagons that ran on rails, while fans and pumps dispersed

An original enamel signpost in the barrack tunnels.
Author's collection

fumes and ensured air circulation. Plans for the construction of a further series of tunnels leading to underground shelters and machine gun turrets at some distance outside Fort Vaux were never implemented. The shaft here is one of the entrances to the new tunnel system. There are other shafts in the rotating turret, observation posts and ditch bunkers and the fact that they are unsecured is one of the reasons why those areas are not open to the public. The well is a few metres from the bottom of this shaft.

On the far side of the shaft a blocked tunnel leads to the wartime entrance outside the ditch. The red line on the walls indicates that this area was strong enough to resist heavy shelling. Today the stairs beyond the shaft lead to the small external blockhouse built after the French retook the fort but they originally provided access to the 'balcony' of the fort, close to the main entrance, and also to the officers' latrines. It was into the cesspits there that Lieutenant Roy threw the documentary archives of Fort Vaux before the surrender.

Internal damage and the eastern Bourges Casemate

From here, return to the corner by the command post and turn right into the eastern tunnel. The German inscriptions on the walls here date from the Second World War. Continue along the tunnel, which would bring you to Ditch Bunker No. 1 if you could follow it all the way. Ahead, note the internal damage caused by the explosion of a sixty-kilogram demolition charge by the Germans before they left Fort Vaux on 2 November 1916. Similar-sized charges were placed in all the underground tunnels, as well as in the observation posts, the powder magazines and the new access tunnel that the Germans had begun to excavate between Ditch Bunker No. 1 and Vaux Hill.

The steps entering the tunnel on the right lead to the eastern Bourges Casemate. The walls ahead are a light version of the massive chicanes that were erected here after the French reoccupied the fort. Between 5 June

Looking into two of the rock tunnels.
Author's collection

and 7 June the machine gun barricade that formed the final French defence of this tunnel stood approximately where these walls stand today.

Covered passage through the eastern tunnel

Pass the walls and continue to the wide area at the top of the steps, then stop. Here, the passage from the inner courtyard (on your left) to the eastern side of the fort (on your right) crossed the tunnel. During the siege this passage was barricaded on both sides. The German flamethrower attack of 5 June was directed against the barricade on the

The powder magazines.
Author's collection

left and, although it was unsuccessful, it led Raynal to pull his men back to the machine gun barricade that formed the final defence of this tunnel. Between 5 June and 7 June the distance between the French defenders of this tunnel and the nearest Germans was roughly the distance between the chicane walls and the blocked-up exit on your left.

Powder magazines (ammunition depot)

Now go down the steps. On the right are the powder magazines which originally housed the shells and explosives needed for the fort's guns. Lights were not allowed in the magazines because of the danger of explosions. Instead, lanterns were placed in the small windows behind enormously thick glass before men wearing felt shoes and clothes without metal fastenings were allowed to enter. The three-section aperture to be seen below one of the windows allowed for ventilation, as powder had to be kept dry. By the end of 1915 the shells and explosives stored here had been removed for use elsewhere and the magazines were empty. During the siege these magazines were used as a temporary morgue. They were rebuilt in the inter-war period.

Troop latrines

These are at the bottom of the stairs on the left. When this fort was built, internal latrines were for emergency use only. There was no external evacuation of waste and the cesspits underneath were cleaned out by specialised companies. During the Battle of Verdun, when it was not possible for troops to go outside to relieve themselves, the cesspits overflowed and conditions here became exceedingly unpleasant. One of the first things the Germans did when they gained control of Fort Vaux was to try to clean out the latrines; when that failed, they were disinfected using enormous quantities of quicklime. Although this avoided a health hazard, the resulting fumes were so powerful that men could only enter the area wearing gas masks. Altogether the experience was so unpleasant that, in the words of one German veteran of the fort, it was fortunate that the men were not very hungry and therefore did

160

Roof damage in the eastern tunnel caused by the explosion of a sixty kilogram demolition charge on 2 November 1916. *Author's collection*

A postwar view of repair work in the eastern tunnel. *Author's collection*

The same view today.
Author's collection

not need to use 'this delightful spot' very often! The partitions between the latrines date from the refurbishment of Fort Vaux during the 1930s.

Beyond the latrines the tunnel continues to Ditch Bunker No. 1. The chicane wall on the left before you reach the grille was built after the battle. By shining a torch through the grille, the damage caused by the

German timbering used to repair a tunnel, which has collapsed again.
Marcus Massing

explosion of the German demolition charge in the magazines on 2 November 1916 can clearly be seen along the right-hand wall. The passage to the ditch bunker is narrow and damp. An unsecured shaft, which takes up half of the tunnel floor, prevents access to the observation post, while another deep shaft blocks access to the ditch bunker. The entrance to the tunnel that the Germans began to dig during the summer of 1916 can be still be seen under the ditch at the bottom of the steps leading to the bunker.

Chapel

From here retrace your steps along the main corridor, passing the command post and the rotating turret and turning right just beyond the cisterns. The small chapel is situated roughly on the site of the two barricades that formed the final defence of this tunnel from 4 June to 7 June. The wall plaques commemorate the events of June 1916. Beyond the chapel the tunnel leads to the western observation post and Ditch Bunker No. 2, which is very badly damaged. By shining a torch through the grille visitors will see that the floor has been dug up, perhaps to provide earth for sandbags. The chicane wall that partially blocks access to the tunnel was built after the battle. It was through this tunnel that both the French and German garrisons left the fort.

Now return to the main corridor and turn right into a straight passage that has been rebuilt. The door half-way along the corridor on the left leads to storerooms. Continue to the corner and stop. On your right the passage to the inner courtyard, which fell in on 5 June 1916, has been walled off. Now turn left. Ahead of you is the passage through which Lieutenant Bénazet and the bugler slipped out in the early hours of 7 June. The double barricade which was opened to let them through stood roughly level with the entrance to the Bourges Casemate. It was here that Lieutenant Müller first entered, saluting Lieutenant Roy and following him into the barracks along the corridor you have just walked.

Western Bourges Casemate

Turn right into the western Bourges Casemate, which was also rebuilt during the 1930s. The flight of steps on the right of the entrance leads to the magazines and store rooms on the lower floor, from where a tunnel runs to Ditch Bunker No. 3. The rebuilt observation post is on the left of the first gun room. The specially adapted 75mm guns – similar to those that stood here until 1915 – are attached to curved guide rails that allowed them to move to left and right. The wall niche at the side of the second room allowed ammunition to be passed up from the magazine below. By 1916 machine guns had replaced the 75s originally standing here. The Germans also had machine guns here and they proved invaluable during the French attempts to retake the fort in October 1916. After the French recaptured the fort, this Casemate was repaired and rearmed with guns similar to those in position today. From here, return to the exit (*Sortie*), which is in the main corridor just before you reach the cisterns.

TOUR NO. 3

A WALK IN THE VAUX SECTOR

Duration: A leisurely two hours
Distance: Three and a half kilometres

This walk takes in Vaux Hill and Fumin Ravine, two sectors of the utmost importance in the fighting for Fort Vaux. It is covered by IGN maps 3112 ET and Blue Series 3212 Ouest. It is likely to be muddy throughout the year. **Walkers should stick to the paths, stay away from holes in the ground and not attempt to enter either of the infantry shelters described here. When walking along the road, be careful to keep to the grass verge.**

This walk begins at the civil cemetery of Vaux-devant-Damloup. To reach the start of the walk, take the D603 from Verdun towards Etain.

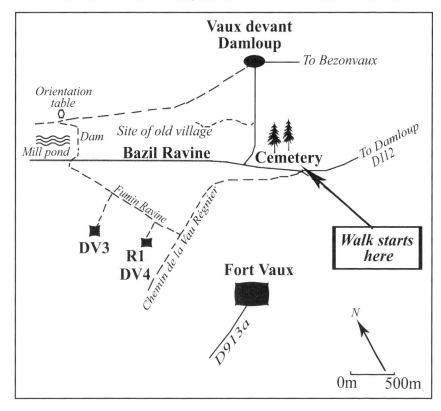

Two German soldiers at the entrance to a Stollen in a quieter area than Vaux Hill. *Marcus Massing*

(NB: On the IGN maps this road is still numbered N3.) The road crosses the Meuse Heights and drops down to a roundabout close to the village of Eix. At the roundabout turn left on the D24 towards Damloup. Drive straight through Damloup and continue to the crossroads with the D112, then turn left following the sign for Verdun. Continue until you reach a modern cemetery on the right-hand side and

The German occupation of the Woëvre Plain to the east of Fort Vaux has left many remains. This is part of a 100 metre long construction in Baty Wood, which is most likely to be post 1916. *Author's collection*

turn right just beyond it at the sign reading '*Vaux village détruit*'. Park by the cemetery and then return to the D112. With the cemetery on your left, walk along the road for approximately 250 metres. The vast extent of the view that comes into sight ahead makes immediately clear the pre-war importance of the ridges on either side of you for defence, observation and signalling. The hill now on your right is Vaux Hill, which was one of the most dreaded sectors of the Verdun front for German troops.

Vaux Hill

At the point where the D112 ceases to run along the edge of the forest and swings left across open fields, turn into the forest on a sandy track between forest blocks 501 and 514. The track meets the road a short distance before a faded sign for a restaurant named *L'Auberge au feu du Bois*. At the junction with the sandy track, stand with your back to Vaux Hill and face ahead. The valley in front of you is Bazil Ravine, which at this point – the eastern end – is roughly 750 metres wide. Vaux stream is marked by the nearest line of trees that crosses the valley from left to right. The destroyed village of Vaux-devant-Damloup stood in the trees to your left front, while the narrow-gauge railway, invisible from here, ran along the base of the hillside opposite. The Hardaumont positions, from which the Germans attacked on 8 March 1916, are at the top of the hillside opposite you. By the time they attacked, the woods here were destroyed, which meant that the French on this side of the valley had a clear view of every move the Germans made.

Now turn right and face across the plain. The German units that captured and held Fort Vaux during the summer of 1916 formed part of 50th Division, which was based in the woods and farms on the plain ahead. When ordered forward, they were first transported by lorry or narrow-gauge railway to within a couple of kilometres from here and then made their way forward on foot. This was no easy matter. The constant bombardment churned the approach to Vaux Hill into a mass of shell holes and broke the banks of the stream on your left, which flooded out into the valley, forcing troops to cross by a limited number of routes that were known to French gunners. It was a race against death every time. The danger of moving up in daylight was so great that men moved only at night, even though the 'ordinary' problems of crossing appallingly difficult and shell-swept terrain were then magnified many times.

Seen from a distance Vaux Hill was a witch's cauldron of light and noise. At night searchlights sent fingers of light across the hillside, coloured rockets lit the sky and everywhere guns roared and spat. With the explosions echoing off the hillsides, the noise was overwhelming. Towards this volcano in continual eruption, troops, heavily laden with supplies needed for the front, had to race forward. Caught in shelling, they dropped their loads, throwing down personal equipment, trenching materials, planking, wire, tools and anything else that they were carrying, pressing themselves into the slimy mud and hoping to survive, before moving on as best they could. Men who did not make it remained lying where they fell, slowly slipping into the mud, as it was too dangerous to bury the dead or even to remove them. As the months went by the approach to Vaux Hill became covered with debris of all sorts, from bones to bloody flesh, twisted weapons, smashed equipment and ammunition. While an approach by night was difficult, it at least spared men the dreadful sight of the decomposing remains of men from their own units who had lain there for weeks.

From here, turn uphill on the sandy track, pass the green and white painted barrier, and continue straight ahead, passing, on the right, a sign reading *Sauf travaux forestiers* and on the left a yellow gas line marker numbered 261. On the IGN maps this track is named the *Chemin de la Vau Régnier*. The steep slopes of Vaux Hill, now on your left, offered cover from incoming shellfire and they were soon covered with camps and *Stollen* – deep underground positions providing storage space for ammunition and supplies as well as shelter for

A rare view from April 1916 of the vitally important entrenchment R1, which blocked the top of Fumin Ravine. *Collection Vieillot*

command posts, dressing stations and men. Anyone caught on Vaux Hill in shelling, regardless of unit, raced to the nearest *Stollen*, which was generally crammed full already, and squeezed himself in until the danger had passed. With so many men inside, the temperature rose to unbearable heights and the air was almost unbreathable. In such circumstances a single direct hit from a heavy shell had catastrophic results and for some veterans being caught inside *Stollen* during shelling was the worst of their experiences.

Having got this far, columns and companies going forward waited for guides to take them up to the fort. However, the guides often disappeared en route or, when they did get through, became lost in the ever-changing landscape of shell craters and debris. In such cases the men had to find their own way forward. With pounding hearts and bathed in sweat, they scrambled over the broken ground in the hope of finding someone who knew the way, scanning the hill for a dark shape that was different and bigger from every other dark shape and hoping against hope that they would eventually reach one of the small openings that led to safety inside the fort.

There are trenches, collapsed dugout entrances and signs of heavy shelling on both sides of the path but they are more visible in winter than in summer. This hillside was so important to the German occupation of the Vaux sector that it is unfortunate that forestry work has destroyed so much of what remained only a few years ago.

Continue along the path, which rises steadily uphill. When you pass gas line marker 266 Fort Vaux is roughly 400 metres to your left and

A quiet day at entrenchment R1 in April 1916. Apart from the odd block of stone or concrete, there is no sign of this 150 metre long position today.
Collection Vieillot

Infantry Shelter DV4 in 2010.
Author's collection

in 1916 it would have been fully visible from here. Continue ahead along the same track for approximately 250 metres and when you reach a sign on the left reading *Sentier de Vaux, Fort de Vaux 1000m*, turn right downhill between forest blocks 502 and 501. A short distance further on you will see a memorial on the right of the track. This commemorates Henri Waechter, aged 23, a machine gunner with the 124th Infantry, who was killed in this area on 3 June 1916. His body was reinterred after the war in front of the Ossuary (plot 8178). His memorial is one of many made after the war by the Renaux firm of monumental masons, which still exists in Verdun. Turn left opposite the memorial at the sign reading *Abri d'Infanterie DV4, 125m* and follow the beaten track to the ruined concrete shelter (DV4), then stop and face downhill, keeping the shelter on your left. Note how steeply the ground falls away in front of you.

A view along the front of DV4 showing how the blast wall protected the entrances.
Author's collection

Infantry shelter DV4 and entrenchment R1

You are now at the top end of Fumin Ravine, a valley of vital importance to the Germans, as it offered sheltered access between Bazil Ravine and Fort Vaux. Unfortunately it was also the site of numerous French infantry strongpoints and, as the woodlands were gradually destroyed, any German attempt to move forward became instantly visible. The fighting for Fumin Ravine began at the end of March 1916 and it quickly became a place of horror. The Germans soon managed to establish themselves on the eastern side of the ravine – to your right front – where they took over and developed former French positions. However, they were prevented from gaining complete control of the ravine by strongly defended French positions on the western side and also from two positions here. These comprised the infantry shelter on your left and a long concrete entrenchment named R1, which stood to the right of the shelter and has completely disappeared.

One of many similar entrenchments built before the First World War, R1 comprised a deep trench 150 metres long that followed the contour of the hillside to your right. The trench was surmounted by a stone and concrete breastwork that was divided by buttresses into recesses in which troops could take shelter. R1 was connected to DV4 by a communication trench and both works were surrounded by wire. During April and May 1916 the Germans managed to drive saps to within fifty metres of R1 but their repeated attacks on the position

Inside a similar infantry shelter, showing fittings for benches along the right hand wall and the archway through to the next room. *Author's collection*

were unsuccessful and by the beginning of June the ravine was carpeted with an appalling litter of corpses, smashed debris and blood-stained belongings.

During the siege of Fort Vaux R1 was held by 8 Company, 101st Infantry, commanded by Captain Charles Delvert, whose gripping account of their experience is a classic of Verdun literature. During that crucial period R1 was not only in the closest possible contact with the Germans but in the direct line of their advance on the fort. Unable to sleep for a moment, tortured by thirst and inadvertently shelled by their own artillery with devastating effect, Delvert and his dwindling band of men held off repeated German attacks from 31 May to 5 June 1916. These assaults were so costly

The memorial plaque to Gustav Schien, which disappeared from DV4 in 2010. *Author's collection*

for the Germans that further attacks were called off and it was only after Fort Vaux had surrendered that R1 was taken and the Germans could turn their attention to DV4.

R1 stood slightly higher than DV4 and the Germans managed to get on to the roof of the shelter without realising that they had reached it. When they did so, they climbed down, banged on the door and shouted that the defenders should surrender. A discussion took place inside and the door opened and shut several times. Finally, one of the Germans stuck his foot in the door and reached in, grabbing a French officer and pulling him outside. With that, all resistance ended.

Now face the front of DV4 but do not attempt to enter it. This strong shelter, one of four identical shelters between Fort Douaumont and Fort Vaux, was built to house a half-company of infantry in two rooms measuring four metres by ten metres. There was a kitchen in a small third room and a latrine outside. Once inside, the men were protected by walls two metres thick and a strong reinforced concrete roof, while the blast wall in front of the shelter – now mostly destroyed – provided cover for the entrances. The lower floor contained a water cistern and the whole area was surrounded by wire. The importance of DV4 made it a constant target for the heaviest German guns, as is clear from the massive damage to the roof to be seen inside. Despite that, it remained an important French strongpoint for months and, during the siege of

Fort Vaux, machine guns in the sandbagged entrances ripped every German attack to shreds.

Front line first aid posts

In a battlefield constantly swept by shellfire, any concrete construction offered safety and shelter, particularly for the wounded, but conditions in such places were awful in the extreme. The rudimentary first aid post at R1, designed to accommodate six to eight wounded, was described by Delvert as a scene of butchery. Inside, a doctor and a priest, their hands covered in blood, dressed wounds as fast as they could by the light of a single candle. It often happened that men who were unable to get inside the tiny shelter were finished off by shells during the night and when the sun rose dead and wounded alike were covered by clouds of flies. The situation in DV4 was no better. Until recently a handsome bronze plaque by the entrance on the left commemorated Lieutenant Gustav Schien, 88th Reserve Infantry Regiment, who died on 2 August 1916, possibly in the first aid post here. Sadly the plaque was stolen during the summer of 2010. Pierre-Marie Coppin (also spelt Copin), 238th Infantry, who is remembered in the nearby memorial under the trees, died in the French attempt to relieve Fort Vaux on 6 June 1916.

Even with Fumin Ravine as overgrown as it is today, the commanding position of R1 and DV4 is clear. It was their resistance during the siege – of which the defenders here may have been unaware – that prevented the Germans from pushing down the western side of Fort Vaux and attempting to surround it. Once captured by the Germans, these positions remained in German hands until November 1916.

Infantry shelter DV3

Now retrace your steps to the memorial for Henri Waechter and turn left downhill. Cross the bottom of the ravine and continue uphill until you see a sign on the left reading *Abri d'Infanterie DV3, 200m*. You will have to watch out for this sign, as only the back of it is visible when you arrive from this direction.

You are now on the western side of Fumin Ravine. Turn left at the sign and follow the path to infantry shelter DV3. The path, which is marked by a solid green circle on a white background, starts by following an old communication trench but soon leaves it and runs steeply uphill through an area of stunted trees, endless shell holes and trenches. When you reach the shelter, face the front but do not attempt to enter.

DV3. *Author's collection*

This shelter was flanked by two infantry entrenchments, which together commanded Fumin Ravine, Bazil Ravine and the destroyed village of Vaux-devant-Damloup. Having failed for weeks to gain control of these positions, the Germans brought two 105mm mountain howitzers to Hardaumont on 31 May 1916 and, after a rapid bombardment, all resistance here ceased. During the summer of 1916 the Germans cut an exit through the rear wall of the shelter to facilitate access from here to Bazil Ravine. They also drove a tunnel into Fumin Ravine from the water cistern, possibly to connect with the many dugouts excavated there. From the left-hand end of DV3 a shallow communication trench runs for some fifty metres to the ruins of a small searchlight shelter. It is not clear from the records whether a searchlight was ever installed here. DV3 remained in German hands until November 1916.

The war memorial of the destroyed village of Vaux-devant-Damloup.
Author's collection

Bazil Ravine and Vaux village

Now return to the main path, turn left and follow it until you reach the D112, then stand by the information board facing across the valley. You are once again in Bazil Ravine, with the Hardaumont positions on the opposite side of the valley. Immediately in front of you is the former village mill pond. To your left Bazil Ravine narrows and links up with several other valleys that lead toward the inner fortress line and Verdun. The old village of Vaux-devant-Damloup, which was completely destroyed during the Battle of Verdun, was situated to

your right front, with the nearest house about 200 metres away. The site of the old village is now completely buried in woodland.

The first German attack on Vaux village took place at the end of February 1916 but it was 8 March before German troops succeeded in gaining a foothold in the houses at the eastern end, about 800 metres to your right. It took another three weeks before all the houses – by now just piles of corpse-strewn rubble – were under their control. Even then, the way to Fort Vaux was not open, as the French still held positions on each side of the valley from which they could pour fire into any German troops pushing down from Hardaumont and uphill to the fort. It was only on 1 June, after another two months of murderous fighting, that the Germans managed to clear the hillsides sufficiently to gain control of the mill dam, which was the shortest route across the valley and the only firm path through an area of impassable marsh. Knowing its importance to the Germans, the French kept the dam under constant fire and, to the unfortunate men who had to cross it during the summer of 1916, the fearsome route was known as the *Todespfad* or Death Path. On all sides the ground was strewn with material jettisoned in the men's haste to reach the other side, including wounded, for whom it was too dangerous to stop. Having reached this side of the valley, they threw themselves into the nearest *Stollen*, of which traces remain on the hillside behind you.

Return via the new village

Visitors who wish to shorten the walk may now return to their cars by turning right and walking along the D112, always remembering to keep

A postcard view of the French 240mm naval gun that stood in Grand Houyers Ravine. *Author's collection*

The road from the new chapel at Vaux village to the civil cemetery. After the war the Verdun battlefield was handed over to the national forestry office and the nine destroyed villages were not rebuilt. The site of the old village of Vaux is in the trees on the left of the road. The memorials to the village and old church are on the right. *Author's collection*

to the grass verge and avoiding traffic. Visitors who prefer to return by a quieter route should cross the dam to the other side of Bazil Ravine and go up the steps to the orientation table. Guy Dussumier Latour, whose death is commemorated halfway across, was a pilot with the French 1st Aviation Group who was killed on 2 June 1916 when his Caudron G4 was shot down in this area. The orientation table has an interesting

Memorial to airman Guy Dussumier Latour, who crashed in his Caudron G4 with his observer, Henri Thévenin, on the first day of the siege of Fort Vaux. *Author's collection*

sketch of the area as seen by German balloon observers before the assault of 21 February 1916, when Fort Douaumont and Fort Vaux would have been visible from where you are standing. The nearby small memorial records the actions of 126 officers and men of the 1st Battalion of *Chasseurs à Pied* (light infantry), who died in the final German assault on Vaux village on 31 March 1916. Note the communication trench running down the hillside between the orientation table and the Chasseurs memorial.

The wide track that passes the orientation table is the embankment for the *Tacot*, the light railway that before the First World War ran from Verdun to Montmedy, a town close to the Belgian border. It was relaid after the Armistice for the purpose of clearing the battlefield and the lines were later taken up. With the stream on your

right, follow the *Tacot* to the modern village of Vaux, which is one kilometre ahead. As you do so, you will pass, on the left, the handsome war memorial which records the names of the civil and military victims of the destroyed village. When you reach the modern village, face the chapel. On the left a steep valley named Grand Houyers Ravine runs uphill to Hardaumont. Before the Battle of Verdun this ravine was the site of a French 24cm naval gun so positioned as to control the railway line and roads on the plain to your right. The gun's existence is recalled in the name of the street to the left of the chapel: *Allée de la Pièce de Marine*: Naval Gun Way. The old railway station was a short way along the road to the right.

With the chapel behind you and the clock tower on your right, return along the road to the cemetery. On the left, roughly half-way along, is the memorial to the destroyed village of Vaux, with a memorial to the old village church beyond it at the field edge. Addressing the passer-by directly, the inscription on the memorial by the road instructs him to 'Tell other nations that this village died to save Verdun and for Verdun to save the world'. The high-flown style underlines the importance of the old village, which blocked access to Bazil Ravine and the connecting valleys that led towards Verdun. This is the only one of the villages destroyed in the Battle of Verdun to be described in such terms.

The original village was situated on the right of the road and visitors wishing to visit the site should follow the path that passes the wooden barrier opposite the memorial, being aware that it will be overgrown and muddy throughout the year. The path ends close to the site of the former village church and a small memorial to a workman killed by an explosion in 1951. If you do not wish to visit the site, continue along the road to the cemetery, which contains a number of French war graves. At the time of writing, the plaques have been removed, perhaps for cleaning. One can only hope that they will soon be returned.

TOUR NO. 4

DRIVING TOUR AROUND FRENCH REAR AREAS

Duration: Five hours, including time for a leisurely visit to the Ouvrage de la Falouse and the nearby caves

Distance: Roughly forty-five kilometres

This tour covers the Voie Sacrée supply road, General Pétain's headquarters at Souilly and medical services at Dugny-sur-Meuse, all sites of major importance to the French effort at Verdun. It also takes in the Ouvrage de la Falouse, which was the last fieldwork to be built at Verdun before the First World War. As there are few cafés or restaurants on this route, it is a good idea to bring a snack or a picnic.

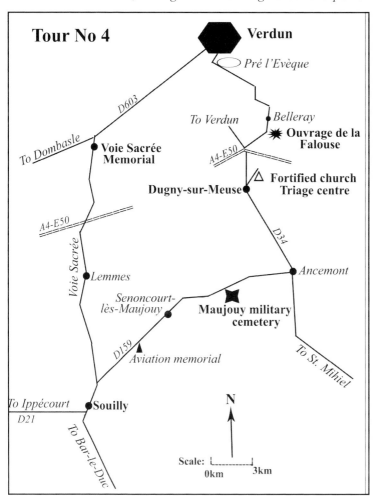

A general map such as Michelin 307 Local (Meurthe-et-Moselle, Meuse, Moselle) or IGN (orange series) Meuse 55 will be useful. For a detailed study of the area I suggest IGN Blue Series 3113 Est Dugny-sur-Meuse and 3213 Ouest Dieue-sur-Meuse. NB: On some maps the D603 may still be numbered N3.

The tour begins in Verdun at the car park of the *Office de Tourisme*, which is on the *Avenue Général Mangin*, close to the city war memorial. This represents five soldiers in the uniforms of 1914–18 who stand with their backs to the wall, symbolizing the 'human rampart' that stopped the German offensive in 1916. A plaque on the wall nearby commemorates the career of General Charles Mangin, who planned the French counter-offensive of October 1916. General Sarrail, who is represented on the plinth across the road from the Mangin plaque, was responsible for the defence of Verdun during the first two years of the war.

The mighty Rodin statue presented to Verdun after the war by the people of Holland.

Author's collection

From here, drive over the bridge towards the old city gate, with its two towers, and follow the road past the Rodin statue, which stands on the right. Entitled 'The Call to Arms', this mighty work was presented to Verdun after the war by the people of Holland. Continue ahead, passing the old St Paul city gate on the left and following the *Avenue Garibaldi* towards the railway station. This is the pinkish-brown building with a clock on the front that you see ahead of you. At the roundabout just before the station area (*Rond-Point des Etats-Unis*) take the third exit into the D603, following the green road signs for *Châlons, Reims, Bar-le-Duc*. The Rond-Point is the site of memorials to two vital military supply routes, the *Voie Sacrée* of 1916 and the *Voie de la Liberté* of 1944, each of which served Verdun. Continue along the D603, which passes through an urban area and crosses over the railway line.

At the 'pencil' roundabout, just after the railway line, take the third exit, still following *Châlons, Reims, Bar-le-Duc*. The road continues through the town for a while before emerging into open country. Continue ahead, passing the extensive industrial area of Baleycourt. The two French 400mm howitzers that shelled Fort Douaumont and Fort Vaux in the run-up to the counter-offensive of 24 October 1916 stood in this area. At the next roundabout take the second exit following signs to *Bar-le-Duc* and *Souilly*. At *Maison Brulée*, which is approximately 500 metres further on, turn sharp left into a rough roadside parking area. The turn comes immediately after a blue road sign on the right reading *Codecom Meuse Voie Sacrée*. Drive uphill to the memorial and face the road.

The *Voie Sacrée* memorial

The German attempt of September 1914 to encircle Verdun damaged the main railway lines into the city and left Verdun dependent on two supply routes: a narrow-gauge railway line named the *Petit Meusien* and the road below the memorial, which links Verdun with Bar-le-Duc.

Known today as the *Voie Sacrée*, or Sacred Way, this road is the most famous supply route used during the Battle of Verdun. Originally less than six metres wide, it was widened in 1915 to allow two vehicles to pass but, as long as the Verdun sector remained quiet, further measures to develop it were deemed unnecessary and at the beginning of 1916 it remained winding and poorly surfaced. On 20 February 1916, just one day before the Germans launched the Battle of Verdun, a regulatory commission took

The memorial to the Voie Sacrée.
Author's collection

control of this road, which was henceforth exclusively reserved for motor transport. On the same day Captain Doumenc, an exceptionally gifted French transport officer, undertook to ensure the daily supply of 2,000 tonnes of goods and equipment and 15–20,000 troops to the Verdun front. Artillery convoys, food and horse-drawn vehicles had to use other routes.

A truck convoy on the Voie Sacrée during the Battle of Verdun. *Tony Noyes*

A similar truck portrayed on the memorial. *Author's collection*

Organizing the road involved dividing the seventy-five kilometres between Bar-le-Duc and Maison Brulée into six administrative units, or cantons. Each one was headed by an officer, who was responsible for keeping the traffic moving and the road repaired at all times. He was also responsible for security, which was ensured by military police, cavalry units and fighter planes. To prevent the road from breaking up under the constant grinding of wheels, quarries were opened nearby and territorial battalions brought in to break the stone

and shovel it under the trucks as they passed. The two- or three-ton vehicles were forbidden to stop or overtake and any truck that broke down was ditched. Troops bound for Verdun were brought to this area, where they disembarked and made the rest of the journey on foot. Supplies were offloaded at dedicated stores dumps along the road. The village of Maison Brulée was the end of the line and the trucks, which travelled in organized convoys, turned round at a specially constructed circle where the modern roundabout stands today. An example of the type of truck that made the journey is to be seen on the battlefield in Fleury Memorial Museum.

One of the kilometre stones on the Voie Sacrée.
Author's collection

During the Battle of Verdun this road was always busy and, until new standard-gauge railway lines could be built, it formed the main access and supply route to the front. Every day, thousands of vehicles ground their way forward, whatever the weather. Traffic jams were frequent and drivers worked for days without a break. The trucks passed at the 'normal' rate of one every fourteen seconds – rising to one every five seconds during particularly desperate times. Between March and June 1916, when a new standard-gauge railway line began to take the pressure off

this road, the monthly traffic on the *Voie Sacrée* exceeded half a million tonnes of supplies and 400,000 troops, in addition to the 200,000 wounded evacuated by ambulance. By December 1916 almost two and a half million men had passed along here. Throughout the First World War no other single route on the Western Front carried as much traffic for as long a period as did the *Voie Sacrée*.

It was both the overwhelming importance of this road and its place in the experience of so many Frenchmen that led the writer Maurice Barrès to name it the *Voie Sacrée*, after the sacred processional road of ancient Rome. The name stuck and after the war each kilometre

One of the sculpted panels on the Voie Sacrée memorial.
Author's collection

of the road was marked by a red and white stone, surmounted by a bronze helmet. The original helmets have all been stolen and the current marker stones, still one kilometre apart, have resin helmets.

The sculpted panels on the memorial commemorate the massive effort to supply Verdun by road, rail and horse-drawn vehicle. The winged wheel on the central pillar is the emblem of the logistics branch of the French army, while the little locomotive is of the type that ran on the *Petit Meusien* railway. This seventy eight kilometre line had been completed before 1914 and, when the battle began, it was being extended and improved. The company that ran it did not have sufficient rolling stock to meet the needs of a major battle but an appeal for narrow-gauge stock from other parts of France swiftly brought locomotives and wagons. The *Meusien*'s main task was to carry food and evacuate wounded and by the end of February 1916, with 800 wagons already available, twenty two trains were running every day. In March the *Meusien* carried 4,000 tonnes of supplies and over 14,000 men, while in June these figures had risen to 10,000 tonnes and almost 75,000 men. While this hardly compared with the tonnages carried by road, it was nevertheless a remarkable effort.

The tour now continues towards Souilly. Before you leave the parking area by the road, note the memorial to Captain Doumenc, who rose to the rank of general officer and is commemorated here as the organizer of the *Voie Sacrée*. If you wish to photograph one of the special kilometre stones, you will find one on the far side of the road, a few metres back in the direction of Verdun **but great care must be exercised in crossing the road here.** More kilometre stones will be seen as you continue the tour to Souilly.

To Souilly

From the parking area, turn left along the *Voie Sacrée*, passing the entrance to the motorway (A4–E50) and continuing straight ahead through Lemmes to Souilly (roughly five kilometres). In 1916 the sides of this road, now so empty and quiet, were lined with camps, workshops, airfields, stores dumps and all the appurtenances of war. Arriving at Souilly, continue into the centre of the village and stop at the *Mairie* (town hall). This handsome detached building, with a double staircase on the outside, stands on the left-hand side of the road by a minor crossroads. Look for the green-painted, ornamental water pump standing on the pavement in front of it. There is a car park behind the *Mairie*. Having parked, return to the roadside.

This was the place chosen by General Pétain to be the headquarters

At Souilly town hall during the Battle of Verdun. In the foreground General Joffre, wearing a kepi with gold braid, talks to President Poincaré of France, who is on the left. General Pétain is on the steps behind Joffre. *Author's collection*

The view down the street from Souilly town hall during the Battle of Verdun. It has not changed much. *Author's collection*

of Second Army during the Battle of Verdun. His arrival to take over command at one minute after midnight on 26 February 1916 is recorded on the marble plaque on the wall under the staircase. Pétain remained here until 1 May 1916, when he moved to command the Group of Armies of the Centre at Bar-le-Duc. Between that date and 21 September 1918 Second Army operations were commanded from here by Generals Nivelle, Guillaumat and Hirschauer respectively. After that date the *Mairie* formed the headquarters of the American First Army, commanded by General John Pershing. George C. Marshall, then a colonel on General Pershing's staff, who was here during the Meuse–Argonne campaign of autumn 1918, described Souilly as 'a depressing little village at best', and added that the almost constant inclemency of the weather did not add to its attractiveness. With the exception of cars and telegraph poles, the view downhill from the *Mairie* has changed little and it is easy to imagine the scene during the Battle of Verdun when, with railway precision, a constant stream of trucks and cars rumbled along this single street. How the scene must have impressed Lieutenant Buffet, brought here to meet General Nivelle and tell in person the story of his escape from Fort Vaux!

The *Mairie* is open to visitors; if the front door is not open, visitors should try the rear. General Pétain's office is on the upper floor and interesting contemporary photographs line the staircase. The bust of General Pétain at the top of the stairs was found in the River Meuse in the 1970s.

The Battle of Verdun had hardly started before General Joffre ordered the construction of a new standard-gauge railway line to supply the front. Work began at both ends and on 21 June 1916 the line, known as *6bis*, was operational. It passed through Souilly, which became the site of huge railway yards, sidings and workshops. The Second Army medical service directorate was also here and other medical services included an important hospital, a surgical centre and an observation camp for German prisoners of war, many of whom arrived from the Eastern Front carrying contagious diseases. The hospital, which was situated alongside the new line and close to a stream, comprised over 1,300 beds and had a sizeable medical staff. Unfortunately, the hospital buildings, which were wooden, have entirely disappeared, as has all trace of the vast railway installations. They stood in open ground on the north side of the D21 from Souilly to Ippécourt, before the road reaches the forest. (Visitors who wish to visit the site, which is now just open fields, should continue downhill from the *Mairie* and take the next right turn at the sign for Ippécourt.)

From Souilly to Dugny-sur-Meuse

Now return to the *Voie Sacrée* and turn back towards Verdun. After approximately 750 metres, fork right on the D159 following signs to Senoncourt and Dieue sur Meuse. During the Battle of Verdun Souilly airfield stood on the right of this road, while hangars stood on the left. Some 1300 metres after the fork a small aviation memorial on the right commemorates Adjutant Gilbert Catteau (pilot) and Lieutenant André Labie (observer) who died in an accident while returning from a night reconnaissance on 29 August 1916. **This is a difficult place to stop, so take great care if you wish to get out and take a photograph.**

From here, continue along the D159 to Senoncourt-lès-Maujouy and drive straight through the village. Continue to a T-junction and turn right, still on the D159, following signs to St Mihiel. After roughly two and a half kilometres you will see a French military cemetery on the right. To visit the cemetery, turn right on to a dirt track that leads to the parking area, but be careful, as this is a difficult, sharp turn originally designed for ambulances coming from the other direction.

Face the farm on the other side of the road. Until August 1918 French field hospital No. 9/2, known as *Petit Maujouy*, stood in the long field to the left of the cemetery between the forest and the road. With 400 beds and a surgical unit, it served as an overflow for the triage centre at Dugny-sur-Meuse, which you will visit later. In late August 1918 this hospital, which was housed in tents and wooden huts, was handed over to the American First Army and became Evacuation

During the Battle of Verdun young Americans driving ambulances like this Model T Ford performed valiant service for France. *Tony Noyes*

American orderlies bringing casualties to the reception hut at Senoncourt-lès-Maujouy. *Author's collection*

Hospital No. 8. More huts were built and from August 1918 to the Armistice the hospital comprised reception and shock wards, X-ray facilities, dental surgeries and numerous operating theatres. A laundry and a mess tent stood by the stream close to the farm. During the St Mihiel and Meuse–Argonne campaigns of autumn 1918 a constant stream of wounded was brought here and specialized surgical teams worked night and day – to give only one example, on 30 September 1918 the six teams on the eleven-hour day shift performed an average of thirty-four operations per team. The American soldiers buried here at the time have either been returned to their families or removed to the American cemetery in Romagne-sous-Montfaucon. Today the cemetery contains the graves of 429 men from over 170 different units, many of whom were from French colonial regiments, reflecting France's history as a colonial power in Africa and elsewhere.

Some American ambulance drivers paid with their lives. Harmon Craig, who died on 16 July 1916, lies in the French military cemetery at Ville-sur-Cousances, southwest of Verdun. *Author's collection*

From here, return to the road and turn right. At the next village, Ancemont, drive ahead until you reach the T-junction with the D34, then turn left towards Dugny-sur-Meuse and Verdun. Continue ahead, passing a huge quarry and cement works on the left. Arriving at Dugny, pass the football ground on your left and continue for approximately 250 metres, staying with the D34 as it bends to the right. Some fifty metres beyond the bend, stop. On the left is a substantial house with a coat of arms over the door and handsome green wrought-iron gates. This is the Chateau Navel.

Medical services at Dugny-sur-Meuse

Situated six kilometres south of Verdun on the Left Bank of the River Meuse, the village of Dugny-sur-Meuse was sufficiently far from the front lines to be safe from shelling and it formed an important logistics and medical centre for a substantial part of the war. The fields and woods around the village offered accommodation for ammunition dumps, artillery and vehicle parks, veterinary hospitals, workshops and anything else needed to sustain a major battle. In the village itself troops filled every house, barn, attic and shed, mixing with those civilians who had refused to leave – old people, children under military age and women replacing men on the farms. Cohabitation between the civilians and the men returning from the front was not always easy. Vacant rooms were requisitioned or simply taken over, men washed themselves and their clothes in the village stream, butchers slaughtered animals in the street and even the street names were changed. Many of the big buildings became hospitals and at the height of the Battle of

Verdun the medical services in Dugny comprised a triage centre in the old church, a surgical unit in the priory behind the church and a hospital for non-transportable patients in the Chateau Navel. Set up in March 1916 to deal with chest and abdominal injuries and gas cases, the Navel hospital also performed operations where necessary. Tents and huts in the grounds behind the house provided extra space and at full

The Chateau Navel. *Author's collection*

capacity this hospital had 150 beds.

During the summer of 1917 the Chateau Navel received the assistance of Miss Yolande de Baye. At the start of the war Miss de Baye had used her private fortune to acquire both surgical and X-ray equipment and a team of nurses and in 1917 she brought her team to

The left side of the nave, where the stretcher cases were lined up.
Author's collection

The nave of Dugny church in 2010. *Author's collection*

this hospital. At that time Dugny was frequently bombed. During an incident on 18 August 1917 three of the nurses were killed and many more were injured, including Miss de Baye. Following that event, the whole nursing team was cited in Army Orders and Miss de Baye received the Cross of the Legion of Honour. A commemorative window dedicated to the nurses who fell here on 18 August 1917 is to be seen in the chapel of the Douaumont Ossuary. The three in question, Miss Piotrowska, Miss Vosdey and Mrs Fichot, are buried in the military cemetery you will visit later.

Now continue along the D34 for approximately 200 metres. Pass the *Rue Briquette* (on the right), cross the small bridge (which at the time of writing has red railings) and turn right into the *Rue Louis Piquet*. At the turn you will see a coloured plan of Dugny on the left. Drive to the far end of the street and stop by the old church with a fortified tower.

The triage centre that operated in this church was served by the medical staff of four field hospitals and as a result it was able to function without interruption. Day and night, ambulances – including some driven by young Americans in the service of the French Red Cross – unloaded their cargoes of mangled flesh in front of the main door, and for many men it was a place of horror and agony that rang with screams and reeked of disinfectant. New patients were examined in the chancel, where doctors dressed wounds and pharmacists gave anti-tetanus injections. Stretcher cases were lined up on the left of the nave while the more lightly wounded waited on the pews. During the German offensive of June 1916 hundreds of wounded and gassed men were brought here – 1140 on 22 June alone – many of whom were later evacuated to other hospitals in the area. On average this church triaged between 7,500 and 8,000 wounded and gassed men per month. Following triage, non-transportable patients requiring surgery were transferred to the Priory, which is the building partially hidden by a high wall at the rear of the church. On average the Priory received sixty five seriously injured men every day. However, as patients arrived there anything up to six days after being wounded, mortality rates sometimes reached as high as 50

A view of the fortified church at Dugny-sur-Meuse with the Priory on the left.
Author's collection

per cent. The military cemetery in the field close to the Priory will be visited later in the tour.

From the church retrace your steps along the street for approximately 200 metres until you see a small lawn set among trees on the left. The building just visible behind the high wall on the far side of the lawn is the Chateau Humbert, which formed the headquarters of the

The former Mairie, or town hall, which served as the Communications HQ for 3 Corps during the Battle of Verdun. *Author's collection*

Verdun Fortified Region during the Battle of Verdun. The Forts Department of Second Army was also based there and, before he took up his post, Major Raynal spent some days there learning about Fort Vaux and visiting other forts in the area.

From here, continue ahead for approximately 200 metres until you reach the new *Mairie*, which is a yellow post-war building, standing on the left, with the words *Mairie* and *Foyer Communal* picked out in red. The handsome building on the other side of the road is the old *Mairie*, which is now an elementary school. During the siege of Fort Vaux, it served as the communications HQ for 3 Corps and it was to this building that Raynal's pigeon messages were sent for a response.

Now return to the D34 and turn right. After approximately 200 metres, stop by the new church, which is on the right. The war memorial records the death of René Didiot, aged 13, who lost a leg one Sunday in March 1916 when a bomb launched from high altitude by a single German plane fell in the middle of a group of territorials on parade, killing and injuring ninety four soldiers and civilians, including young René, who died two days later.

Continue towards Verdun. Just before the road crosses the railway, take the right fork towards the military cemetery at the sign reading *Dugny s/M* and showing a French helmet on a red, white and blue background. The military cemetery contains 1,815 graves from a great many regiments, including a small number from the Second World War. Roughly half way down the cemetery, just to the right of the centre, is a memorial to the doctors, pharmacists and stretcher-bearers of the 73rd Division who were killed in the fire in Tavannes railway tunnel on 4 September 1916. Throughout the Battle of Verdun this strongly built railway tunnel offered shelter and accommodation to thousands of men, as well as space for medical services and stores. On

189

4 September an explosion at the eastern end started a fire. The tunnel was 1300 metres long and as flames and smoke spread, sucked in by the ventilation shaft in the middle, panic set in. The heat was so intense that rescue teams could not get in and the fire burned for several days. The official death toll of 500 included 101 men from the divisional stretcher-bearer group, including the senior doctor, four pharmacists and six dentists. The three nurses killed in the bombing of the Chateau Navel in 1917 are buried in Graves 200, 249 and 251. These are to be found on the extreme left of the cemetery in the sixth, seventh and eighth rows from the bottom, from where a good view of the Priory and the fortified church can be obtained.

From Dugny to Belleray

Now return to the D34 and turn right. After roughly one kilometre the D34 passes under the A4 motorway. Immediately after the motorway bridge, turn right on the D301 towards Belleray. Follow the road as it crosses the railway line and, just beyond the brow of the hill, turn sharp right along a signposted, stony track towards the *Ouvrage de la Falouse*. This modern, reinforced concrete fieldwork was the last to be built at Verdun and it formed part of the main line of resistance on the Left Bank of the River Meuse. It was one of the positions open to Raynal, who, having been appointed to command Fort Vaux, came here several times as part of his training. During the Battle of Verdun La Falouse, which covers an important road, several Meuse bridges and the gap between two major Left Bank forts (Dugny and Haudainville), served only as a barracks and supply depot but it would have become more important in the case of a withdrawal to the Left Bank. The fieldwork, which features life-size models of soldiers with accurate uniforms and equipment in scenes of military life, has recently been restored and is open to the public (the opening times are listed in the Useful Addresses section of this book). It is very well worth a visit.

From here, return to the D301, turn right and drive downhill into Belleray. At the crossroads by the church, just before the bridge, turn right into the *Rue Haute*, drive along to the military cemetery and stop.

From the start of the Battle of Verdun this little village – almost the same size as it is today – was of vital importance. With German long-range guns hammering Verdun, the passage of troops and supplies across the River Meuse by

The entrance to the Ouvrage de la Falouse in 2009.
Author's collection

190

the city bridges was slow and unreliable. As a result the bridge at Belleray took on increased importance, as it was one of the few river crossings close to the front to be out of range of German artillery. It also allowed troops and supplies to reach the Vaux sector without going through the city, so from 1916 to the end of the war the bridge saw uninterrupted traffic. This was tightly regulated; the bridge was reserved for wheeled vehicles, while troops and cavalry used one of the seven lighter crossings thrown over the river by the engineers, who had a permanent base here. During that time this village swarmed with men, vehicles and horses. There were thousands of horses here, with an important veterinary service and an abattoir for animals that could not be saved.

Ambulances bringing wounded from the Vaux sector to the hospitals at Dugny came through Belleray, where men who had died en route were taken off and buried. Among the 1,234 men from many regiments who lie here is Second Lieutenant Louis-François Franchet-d'Espèrey, whose father, General Franchet d'Espèrey, was known to British troops as Desperate Frankie. He is buried on the left-hand side of the cemetery in the eighth row from the bottom.

A view of two of the impressive Grottes de la Falouse. *Author's collection*

Roughly two kilometres further along the road the former limestone caves and quarries known as the *Grottes de la Falouse* were used as stabling and provided shelter throughout the war. If you wish to visit the caves, which are quite spectacular and extend along the river for several hundred metres, you have to continue on foot along the road to the *Ferme de la Falouze*, then turn right at the footpath sign just before the farm gates and follow the grassy path to a sign reading *Accès*

A wartime photo of the River Meuse in flood. Even today, winter floods still fill the valley. Such conditions would have presented a formidable obstacle to any German advance. *Tony Noyes*

interdit dans les grottes. Here the path, which has wooden handrails, drops down to the caves. **This area is open to the public and access is free but visitors should stay on the path and observe the signs prohibiting entrance to the caves.**

Return to your car by the same route, then drive to the crossroads in the centre of the village and turn right. Cross the bridge and when you reach the other side of the valley – which annual flooding would have made an impassable obstacle to a German advance – turn left along a very bumpy road that winds uphill to the junction with the *Boulevard Stratégique*. **The junction features a small, temporary roundabout at which care is needed.** Turn left downhill (being aware of the speed camera). The lake that comes into view on the right after you have crossed the River Meuse is *Pré l'Evêque*, from where water was pumped to Fort Vaux after it was recaptured. Cross another little river and continue to the road junction ahead, which is known as the *Carrefour des Maréchaux* and features a number of statues of Marshals of France. Here take the right fork into the *Avenue du 5ème RAP*, following signs for *Centre Ville* and *Citadelle Souterraine*. Ahead you will see the massive walls of the Citadel and the old *Porte Neuve* city gate. Pass the gate and turn into the car park on the left. Park as close as you can to the *Porte Neuve* gate and walk back to the line of four statues closest to the road junction you have just passed. These are the only First World War marshals to feature here and they include General Franchet d'Espèrey. General Pétain, who became a Marshal of France in November 1918 and was fated to arrange an armistice with the Germans in 1940, is not among them. As you return to your car, note on the right, just before the *Porte Neuve*, the memorial to the medical services at Verdun. The plaque, which features a quotation from Baron Percy, Inspector-General of Medical Services and Surgeon-in-Chief of the French Armies during the French Revolution and the Empire, exhorts medical staff to 'Go where the nation and humanity call you'.

The Citadel, which was designed by Vauban,

One of the statues of Marshals of France at the Carrefour des Maréchaux. Although General Pétain's name does not appear on any of the statues, this one bears a surprising resemblance to him. *Author's collection*

Louis XIV's great military engineer and built in the late seventeenth century, was originally the central defensive stronghold of this city and during the Napoleonic Wars it served as a prison for captured Royal Navy officers. In the late nineteenth century the original Citadel was greatly extended by the excavation of several kilometres of wide underground tunnels, which are behind the massive walls you see today. Further tunnels were dug shortly before the outbreak of war in 1914. The underground Citadel became a logistic and supply centre of enormous importance and during the Battle of Verdun the tunnels offered shelter and accommodation to troops, staff officers, medical and municipal services. Most of the regiments that took part in the Battle of Verdun passed through it. The Unknown Soldier, who lies under the Arc de Triomphe in Paris, was selected here from eight unidentified French soldiers taken from different sectors of the Western Front. His coffin was carried out through the doorway of the *Galleries Guinot*, which you will find in the corner at the far left of the car park. If you look carefully, you will see the name of the galleries cut in the stone above the double steel doors. The remaining seven unidentified soldiers were buried in Verdun. They surround the central cross in the *Faubourg Pavé* military cemetery on the *Avenue du Maréchal Joffre*. The cemetery is easily recognized by the six field guns that stand close to the entrance.

Now turn left out of the car park and drive towards the flagpoles

The central cross in the Faubourg Pavé cemetery. *Author's collection*

ahead, which mark the visitor entrance to the Citadel. Beyond them you will see a substantial archway and, a short distance further along on the left, a long pale-coloured building, part of which has two floors. This is all that remains of the former military pigeon loft. The small square windows in the upper floor were originally the entrance hatches used by the pigeons. It was to this building that Fort Vaux's last carrier pigeon returned on 4 June 1916, dying soon after its arrival.

At the next roundabout continue straight ahead into the *Rue du Rû*, following signs to *Centre Ville*. You are now in a one-way system. Passing a car park on your right, keep straight on over a minor roundabout and continue until you reach a T-junction, where you have to turn right. Cross the bridge over the river and turn immediately left along the *Quai de la République* towards the city war memorial, which you will see ahead. The tour ends at the car park of the *Office de Tourisme*.

Waterfront ruins in Verdun after the Battle of Verdun. *Author's collection*

SELECT BIBLIOGRAPHY

FRENCH SOURCES

On Fort Vaux

Monographie du Fort de Vaux, contained in *Verdun et ses forts pendant la guerre, General G. Benoît,* 1929 (Archives du Mémorial de Verdun)

De l'Oppidum à l'Enfouissement. L'Art de la Fortification à Verdun et sur les marches de l'Est, Conference Papers, Mémorial de Verdun (Fleury-devant-Douaumont, 1995), especially:

> *La Construction de la Carapace en béton du Fort de Vaux - 1888*, LEP Freyssinet/Jean-Pierre Iscla

> *La réorganisation des Forts de Verdun pendant la Bataille de 1916*, Martin Barros

> *Le Drame du Fort de Vaux*, Colonel Raynal, Frémont, Verdun (Les Editions Lorraines, 1935)

> *Avec les Honneurs de la Guerre, Souvenirs du Fort de Vaux*, P.-A. Roy, Paris (Editions Bernard Graset, 1938)

War Diaries *(Reference numbers given in brackets)*

> *63ᵉ division d'infanterie* (26 N 382/1)

> *101ᵉ régiment d'infanterie* (26 N 674/2)

> *124ᵉ division d'infanterie* (26 N 425/1)

> *142ᵉ régiment d'infanterie* (26 N 693/15)

> *347ᵉ régiment d'infanterie* (26 N 758/3)

> Fort Souville (26 N 72/20)

> Fort Tavannes (26N 72/21)

On the Battle of Verdun

Les Armées Françaises dans la Grande Guerre, Service Historique, Ministère de la Guerre, Tome IV: Verdun et la Somme, Vols. 1, 2 and 3 (Paris, Imprimerie Nationale, 1926)

GERMAN SOURCES

On Fort Vaux

Schlachten des Weltkrieges, Vol. 14: *Die Tragödie von Verdun 1916 –*
Part II – *Das Ringen um Fort Vaux,* (Oldenburg/Berlin, Verlag Gerhard
Stalling, 1928)

Die Kämpfe um die Feste Vaux von Mitstreitern Geschildert,
Herausgegeben von der 'Feldgrauen', Illustrierten Kriegszeitschrift
der 50. Infanterie-Division 1916.

Regimental histories

*Das Füsilier-Regiment General Ludendorff (Niederrheinisches) Nr.
39,* Franz v. Rudorff (Berlin, Reinhold Kühn A.G., 1925)

Das Paderborner Infanterie-Regiment (7.Lothring.) Nr. 158, Hanns
Möller (Berlin, Verlag Bernard & Graefe, 1939)

*Das 4. Unter-Elsässische Infanterie-Regiment Nr. 143 im Frieden und
im Weltkrieg, Band II,* Fritz Rust (Berlin, Verlag Bernard & Graefe,
1938)

*Das 5. Westfälisches Infanterie-Regiment Nr. 53 im Weltkrieg
1914–1918,* Herbert Maillard (Zeulenroda in Thuringia, Bernhard
Sporn, 1939)

*Das 8. Württembergische Infanterie-Regiment Nr. 126 Grossherzog
Friedrich von Baden im Weltkrieg 1914–1918,* Generalmajor a.D.
Glück and Generalmajor a.D. Wald (Stuttgart, Christian Belfer A.G.,
Verlagsbuchhandlung, 1929)

On the Battle of Verdun

Der Weltkrieg 1914–1918, Vol. 10: *Die Operationen des Jahres 1916;*
Vol. 11: *Die Kriegführung im Herbst 1916 und im Winter 1916/17*
(Reichsarchiv/Kriegsministerium, Berlin, E.S. Mittler & Sohn, 1938)

FURTHER READING

These works are suggested in addition to those listed in the Select Bibliography.

On the Battle of Verdun

In English:

The Price of Glory, Alistair Horne (London, Macmillan & Co. Ltd, 1962)

German Strategy and the Path to Verdun, Robert T. Foley (Cambridge University Press, 2005)

Verdun, Marshal Pétain (London, Elkin Mathews & Marrot Ltd, 1930)

Education before Verdun, Arnold Zweig (New York, Viking, 1936)

Fort Douaumont – Verdun, Christina Holstein (Battleground Europe series; Barnsley, Pen & Sword Books, 2002)

Walking Verdun: A Guide to the Battlefield, Christina Holstein (Battleground Europe series; Barnsley, Pen & Sword Books, 2009)

In French:

Combattre à Verdun, Vie et souffrance quotidiennes du soldat 1916–1917, Gérard Canini (Presses Universitaires de Nancy, 1988)

Verdun: les Forts de la Victoire, Guy Le Hallé (Paris, Citédis, 1998)

Verdun 1916, Jacques Péricard (Nouvelle Librairie de France, 1947)

Verdun, Jacques-Henri Lefebvre (Paris, Editions du Mémorial [1996])

Le Service de santé de l'Armée Française, Verdun 1916, Dr Jean-Jacques Schneider (Metz, Editions Serpenoise, 2007)

In German:

Verdun: Die Schlacht und der Mythos, German Werth (Augsburg, Weltbild Verlag, 1990)

Verdun 1916, Hermann Wendt (Berlin, E.S. Mittler, 1931)

Verdun – Das Grosse Gericht, P.C. Ettighoffer (Gütersloh, Bertelsmann, 1936)

General background

My War Experiences, Crown Prince William of Germany (London, Hurst & Blackett, 1922)

Paths of Glory: the French Army 1914–1918, Anthony Clayton (London, Cassel Military, 2003)

BATTLEFIELD GUIDEBOOKS

There are still few English-language guides to the Battle of Verdun. The Michelin Guide, *Verdun and the Battles for its Possession*, first produced in 1919 and reprinted in 1994 by G.H. Smith & Sons, Easingwold, York, England, is interesting but has little detail. Verdun and the wider area are covered by Major and Mrs Holt's guide to *The Western Front – South,* published by Pen & Sword Books, UK, and by *A historical tour of Verdun* by Jean-Pascal Soudagne and Remi Villagi, published by *Editions Ouest-France* in three languages. My two previous books, *Verdun – Fort Douaumont* and *Walking Verdun*, both published by Pen & Sword Books, UK, offer detailed information about the most important fort in the Verdun system and provide a general walkers' guide to the battlefield.

Visitors who read French will find much interesting information about Verdun in *Première Guerre Mondiale des Flandres à l'Alsace*, published by Editions Casterman in 1996. Although out of print, it is worth looking for a second-hand copy of this book, as it deals with the political background to the war and the leading personalities as well as covering the fighting on the Western Front as a whole. Relevant German publications include the *Militärgeschichtlicher Reiseführer, Verdun,* by Horst Rohde and Robert Ostrovsky (Verlag E.S. Mittler & Sohn, Hamburg, Berlin, Bonn) and *Spurensuche bei Verdun: Ein Führer über die Schlachtfelder* by Kurt Fischer and Stephan Klink (Bonn, Bernard & Graefe Verlag, 2000).

An excellent recent publication, which contains an extensive section on Verdun and the surrounding area, is *Militärgeschichtlicher Reiseführer zu den Schlachtfeldern des Ersten Weltkrieges: Lothringen und Elsass* by Markus Klauer (2009), ISBN 3-9807648-4-2, www.weltkriegesbuch.de

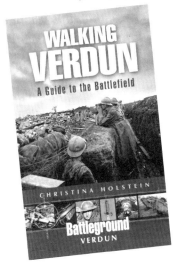

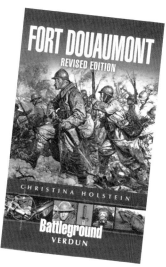

SHORT GLOSSARY

75mm gun – A French 3-inch calibre, quick-firing artillery piece.

Caponier – A strong position in the ditch with internal communication into the main work. Caponiers were provided with loopholes for ditch defence.

Glacis – An area of smoothly sloping ground outside the ditch and entirely surrounding the fort. It was kept clear of all forms of cover so as to afford clear fields of fire in all directions.

Infantry entrenchment – A rifle pit of masonry or cast concrete, often with a metal shield, which may also have recesses for shelter. Such entrenchments were 100–150 metres long.

Parapet – a continuous wall placed on the superstructure of the fort to provide cover for infantry using small arms.

Pioneers – German specialist troops with various skills including field fortification. Those accompanying the infantry were trained in infantry tactics and advanced with the leading waves, clearing away wire and other obstacles.

Sappers – As referred to in this book, these were French soldiers involved in the building and repairing of fortifications.

Storm pioneers – German specialist troops accompanying assault units and specially trained to deal with fixed fortifications.

Zouaves – Light infantry recruited from Frenchmen in France's North African possessions.

USEFUL ADDRESSES

The Verdun tourist offices may be contacted in English. Despite the different addresses, they are almost opposite one another.

Maison du Tourisme, Address: BP 60232, Place de la Nation, 55106 Verdun Cedex.
Tel. + 33 3 29 84 14 18, fax + 33 3 29 84 22 42
Email: verduntourisme@wanadoo.fr
www.en.verdun-tourisme.com
Office de Tourisme, Address: Pavillon Japiot, Ave. Général Mangin, 55100 Verdun.
Tel. + 33 3 29 84 55 55, fax + 33 3 29 84 85 80.
Email : tourisme@cc-verdun.fr
www.tourisme-verdun.fr/

BATTLEFIELD SITES

Please note that opening times may change without warning. At the time of writing visiting times are as follows:

Fort Vaux

Outside: Any time.
Inside: February–March and October–November from 10–5.
April and September from 10–5.30.
May–August from 10–6.30.
December from 10–4.30.
Closed mid-December to end of January.

Fort Douaumont

Outside: Any time.
Inside: February–March and November–December from 10–5.
April and September from 10–6.
May–August from 10–6.30.
October from 10–5.30.
Closed mid-December to end of January.

Mémorial de Verdun (Fleury Memorial Museum)

Address: 1 Ave. Du Corps Européen, 55100 Fleury-devant-Douaumont.
Tel. + 33 3 29 84 35 34, fax + 33 3 29 84 45 54.
http://www.memorial-de-verdun.fr/
1 February–14 March from 9–12 and 2–6.
15 March–11 November from 9–6.
12 November–18 December from 9–12 and 2–6.
Closed 19 December–1 February.

The Ossuary

Address: 55100 Douaumont, France.
Tel. + 33 3 29 84 54 81, fax + 33 3 29 86 56 54.
http://www.verdun-douaumont.com
January closed.
February and December from 2–5.
March and November from 9–12 and 2–5.
April–August from 9–6.
September from 9–12 and 2–6.
October from 9–12 and 2–5.30.

Ouvrage de la Falouse

Address: Lieu-dit Le Plat d'Houillon, 55100 Dugny-sur–Meuse, France.
Tel: 06.83.27.13.34. Email: ouvragedelafalouse@orange.fr

GPS: N4907.3137/E00524 0371
March–September from 9–6.
October–February from 9.30–12 and 2–4.
Other times by appointment.

Verdun City Sites
Monument de la Victoire

Place de la Libération, Verdun
The imposing Monument to Victory and to the Soldier of Verdun takes the form of a cloaked and helmeted warrior thrusting his sword into the ground against the invader. The crypt under the monument is open daily from approximately 9.30–11.30 and from 2–6 every day. Entrance is free. In addition to an alphabetical list of all French troops who were awarded the *Médaille de Verdun*, the crypt houses the first volume of the *Livre d'Or*, which records the names of every French soldier who fought at Verdun. The remainder of the *Livre d'Or* is held in the *Mairie* (town hall).

Centre Mondial de la Paix (World Peace Centre)
Address: BP 183, 55105 Verdun Cedex, France.
http://www.centremondialpaix.asso.fr/
Tel. + 33 3 29 86 55 00, fax + 33 3 29 861514.

The World Peace Centre, situated in the former Bishop's Palace next to the Cathedral, houses permanent and temporary exhibitions on the theme of war and peace, liberty and human rights.
Open daily except Monday from 9.30–12 and 2–6. July and August 9.30–7.

Citadelle Souterraine (Underground Citadel)
Address: Avenue du 5ème R.A.P., Verdun, France.
Tel. + 33 3 29 86 14 18, fax + 33 3 29 84 22 42.
January closed.
December, February and March from 10–12 and 2–5.
April, May, June and September from 9–6.
July–August from 9–7.
October–November from 9.30–12.30 and 2.30–5.30.
Closed from 21 December–1 February.

GRAVE LOCATION

French soldiers

Secteur des Sépultures de Guerre de la Direction Interdépartementale des Anciens Combattants.
Address: 13 rue du 19ème BCP, 55100 Verdun, France.
Email : diracmetz@wanadoo.fr.
Tel. +33 3 29 86 02 96, fax : 03.29.86.33.06.

German soldiers

Volksbund Deutsche Kriegsgräberfürsorge (SESMA).
Address: Werner-Hilpert-Str.2, 34112 Kassel, Germany.
www.volksbund.de
Email: info@volksbund.de

ARCHIVES

French archives

Service Historique de la defense
Address: Château de Vincennes, Ave. de Paris, 94306 Vincennes CEDEX, France.
Tel.: +33 1 41 93 43 90
http://www.servicehistorique.sga.defense.gouv.fr/

German archives

BundesMilitärarchiv
Address: Wiesentalstraße 10, D-79115 Freiburg, Germany.
www.bundesarchiv.de

ACKNOWLEDGEMENTS

In writing this book I have been greatly helped by the generosity of friends who gave their time, expertise and resources to help me. The responsibility for any errors or omissions is mine alone. My thanks go first to Mme Isabelle Remy of the *Mémorial de Verdun* for maps, books and other resources, and to Mme Claire Ben Lakhdar-Kreuwen, Director and Chief Librarian of the Verdun Library, for permission to consult the plans of Fort Vaux contained there. Mme Isabelle Nourry of the *Conseil Général de la Meuse* allowed me to explore those parts of Fort Vaux normally closed to visitors, where I was accompanied by M. Julien Coquet, expert guide at Fort Vaux, who answered many questions. I am also grateful to Dr Bruno Frémont for showing me around the Château Navel, Dugny-sur-Meuse, and to Mme Léa Brix, who generously lent original photos and shared her memories of veterans of the siege. Burleigh Randolph helped with comments on the first chapters, Marcus Massing, Tom Gudmestad and Barthélemy Vieillot supplied photos from their personal collections, while Jan Carel Broek Roelofs kindly allowed me to use the wonderful photographic archive of the late H.P. von Müller. Last, but absolutely not least, love and thanks go to my daughter Isabella, who accompanied me on early explorations in the thick woods around Fort Vaux, and to my husband Tony Noyes, whose deep understanding of the Battle of Verdun illuminated my research every step of the way.

Christina Holstein

Kent, April 2011

INDEX

The Citadel, central redoubt of the fortress city of Verdun, seen from the air.

A

Alirol, Lieutenant	85
Albagnac, Lieutenant	86

B

Bazil Ravine	37, 43 - 45, 166, 173
Bazy, Lieutenant	85
Belleray	190 - 192
Bellmann Lieutenant	123
Bénazet, Lieutenant	103 - 104, 142, 150, 163
Buffet, Léon	82, 89 - 90, 131, 142, 183

C

Chateau Navel	186
Coste, Joseph	103, 132, 142, 163
Crown Prince William of Germany	41, 44, 111, 119

D

Doumenc, Captain	179
Dugny-sur-Meuse	186 - 189
DV3 172 - 173	
DV4 169, 170 - 171	

F

Fretté, Sergeant	90, 132
Fort Douaumont	33, 145
Fumin Ravine	164, 170 - 172

G

Galopin turret	147 - 149
Generals:	
French:	
Coutenceau	29
Herr	32
Joffre	32, 97
de Lardemelle	122
Lebrun	69, 75
Mangin	119, 122
Nivelle	89, 92, 113, 115
Pétain	47, 113, 151
Tatin	58
German:	
Schmidt von Knobelsdorf	46
von Bahrfeldt	46

von Deimling	57, 121
von Engelbrechten	111, 116
von Falkenhayn	33, 47, 119
von Guretzky-Cornitz	38, 41
von Gündell	36
von Mudra	45
Gillhausen, Captain	70, 93 - 4, 108, 140
Grottes de la Falouse	191 - 192

H

| Hardaumont | 36 - 37, 141, 145 |
| Hindenburg, Field Marshal Paul von | 119 |

K

| Kaiser William II | 33 |

M

Military Units: French	
Army:	
Second	34, 47
Corps:	
III	69
Division:	
74th	122 - 3
124th	58
Regiment:	
53rd Infantry	56
101st Infantry	58
142nd Infantry	58
2nd Zouaves	112
Moroccan Colonial Infantry	112
Military units: German	
Army:	
Fifth	33, 41
Corps:	
XV	57
V Reserve	36
Division:	
6th Reserve	39, 42
9th Reserve	38, 42
50th	111, 117
Regiment:	
19th Reserve	38, 42

39th Fusiliers	69, 116
53rd Infantry	8, 57, 116
126th Infantry	69, 116
143rd Infantry	117
158th Infantry	57, 59, 69
192nd Infantry	123
Battalion:	
20th Reserve Pioneers	62
Company:	
100th Pioneers	124
Maginot Line	11, 130
Müller, Werner, Lieutenant	8, 103 - 8, 140, 150, 163

O

Ouvrage de la Falouse	190

P

Petit Maujouy (hospital)	184 - 185

R

Rackow, Lieutenant	59, 62, 116
Raynal, Major	8, 50 - 53, 97, 131, 155
R1	167, 168, 170 - 171
Rosencrantz, Captain	124, 125
Roy, A.P., Lieutenant	8, 82, 153, 163
Ruberg, Lieutenant	62 - 64

S

Souilly	181 - 183

T

Tabourot, Georges, Captain	59

V

Vaux-devant-Damloup	164, 174, 176
Vaux Hill	166 - 168
Verdun Citadel	193
Voie Sacrée	179 - 181

W

Water cisterns	78 - 79, 152 - 153